THE EVERYTHING®
PANINI PRESS COOKBOOK

Dear Reader,

Have you ever been to a trendy café or coffee shop and marveled over the items on the menu board? Did you wonder to yourself, "Why can't I make sandwiches like that at home and why aren't they just as delicious?" Well, stop wondering and start preheating your panini press!

You can make delicious panini in the comfort of your own home any time you want. You don't need exotic ingredients or fancy equipment. All it takes is a panini press and the willingness to try something new.

But if you just use your panini press for making panini, you're not using it to its full potential. You can make desserts, steaks, seafood, hors d'oeuvres, and even wontons with a panini press. It's time you started fully utilizing this valuable kitchen tool.

So if mouth-watering meats, cheeses, and vegetables heated and pressed between crispy and chewy bread sounds like your idea of an excellent meal, then this book is just what you've been looking for.

Have a panini today!

Anthony Tripodi

Welcome to the EVERYTHING® Series!

These handy, accessible books give you all you need to tackle a difficult project, gain a new hobby, comprehend a fascinating topic, prepare for an exam, or even brush up on something you learned back in school but have since forgotten.

You can choose to read an Everything® book from cover to cover or just pick out the information you want from our four useful boxes: e-questions, e-facts, e-alerts, and e-ssentials.

We give you everything you need to know on the subject, but throw in a lot of fun stuff along the way, too.

We now have more than 400 Everything® books in print, spanning such wide-ranging categories as weddings, pregnancy, cooking, music instruction, foreign language, crafts, pets, New Age, and so much more. When you're done reading them all, you can finally say you know Everything®!

QUESTION

Answers to common questions

FACT

Important snippets of information

ALERT

Urgent warnings

ESSENTIAL

Quick handy tips

PUBLISHER Karen Cooper

DIRECTOR OF ACQUISITIONS AND INNOVATION Paula Munier

MANAGING EDITOR, EVERYTHING® SERIES Lisa Laing

COPY CHIEF Casey Ebert

ASSISTANT PRODUCTION EDITOR Jacob Erickson

ACQUISITIONS EDITOR Lisa Laing

ASSOCIATE DEVELOPMENT EDITOR Hillary Thompson

EDITORIAL ASSISTANT Ross Weisman

EVERYTHING® SERIES COVER DESIGNER Erin Alexander

LAYOUT DESIGNERS Colleen Cunningham, Elisabeth Lariviere, Ashley Vierra, Denise Wallace

Visit the entire Everything® series at *www.everything.com*

THE EVERYTHING

PANINI PRESS COOKBOOK

Anthony Tripodi

Adams Media

New York   London   Toronto   Sydney   New Delhi

The book is dedicated to my family:
Cathy, Max, and Alexa.
They're the best thing since sliced bread.

Aadamsmedia

Adams Media
An Imprint of Simon & Schuster, Inc.
57 Littlefield Street
Avon, Massachusetts 02322

An Everything® Series Book.

Everything® and everything.com® are registered trademarks of Simon & Schuster, Inc.

ADAMS MEDIA and colophon are trademarks of Simon and Schuster.

For information about special discounts for bulk purchases, please contact Simon & Schuster Special Sales at 1-866-506-1949 or business@simonandschuster.com.

The Simon & Schuster Speakers Bureau can bring authors to your live event. For more information or to book an event contact the Simon & Schuster Speakers Bureau at 1-866-248-3049 or visit our website at www.simonspeakers.com.

Manufactured in the United States of America

12 2020

Library of Congress Cataloging-in-Publication Data has been applied for.

ISBN 978-1-4405-2769-2
ISBN 978-1-4405-2781-4 (ebook)

Contents

Acknowledgments

I have always wanted to write a book but never realized how much work and support is required to actually get it done. I would like to extend a special thanks to my family for being my guinea pigs and trying all those panini. Especially my daughter Alexa, who is always up for a snack. And for also making do without me while I tapped away at the keyboard during some important family events.

And thanks to Lisa Laing, who had to hear the phrase "I need more time" way too often.

Without the joint effort of all those involved, this book would not have been possible.

Introduction

THE ANSWER TO THE world's most popular question, "What's for dinner?" (or lunch or even breakfast) is often a sandwich. And, unfortunately, it's usually the same kind of sandwich over and over again. Eating the same boring sandwiches day in and day out can become monotonous for some. And for those people, it's a good thing that there are panini.

Making a hot panini instead of a regular sandwich is a great way to shake up your routine and add some fun into your meals. Hot, crispy bread and a variety of ingredients beats the heck out of a peanut butter and jelly on white bread.

Panini are easy to make. All you need is a panini press. You may already own a panini press that's been sitting unused in a closet somewhere. Perhaps you received it as a gift for your wedding or at a shower. Maybe you even used your panini press when you first got it. However it came to be in your possession, it's time to start using it. Clear a space off on your counter right now. Go ahead and move the smoothie maker or the vegetable juicer into the closet and start using that panini press as much as possible.

And if you don't already own a panini press, what are you waiting for? It's one of those inexpensive kitchen appliances that everyone should have. Sandwich presses used to be so large and expensive that only restaurants would buy them, but now they are a very popular home appliance. There's a huge selection of panini presses out there, with many different features and styles. There's bound to be one that suits your needs.

You may think that panini are limited to Italian cuisine, but that's not true at all. Even though the panini is of Italian origin, it has become popular all over the world. And now you'll find many different cuisines influencing panini sandwiches. Chinese wonton wrappers can be filled with all of your favorite ingredients and cooked on the panini press. If you think all the best panini are made with Italian ingredients, you should try a taco panini wonton served with salsa and sour cream for dipping. It's sure to change your mind.

Panini can also make for some great party food. There are recipes in this book for cocktail party panini sandwiches. The only difference between a regular panini and a panini hors d'oeuvre is the strategic use of an ordinary pizza cutter. Just slice that panini into bite-sized pieces and start handing them out with a cocktail napkin. Or put those panini slices out in a chafing dish to stay warm and let your guests choose their favorite dipping sauces for dunking. Sometimes you may even want to skip the bread and use your panini press to grill vegetables, meats, or seafood.

Let this book be your guide to the world of the panini press. Start with these recipes, but don't stop there. Come up with your own variations. Just by changing the bread in a panini recipe you can dramatically impact the flavor. Try different cheeses, add different spreads, swap out those cold cuts. Use your imagination and enjoy yourself.

CHAPTER 1

Panini Basics

If you look up the definition of the word *panini* in a dictionary, it will probably say something like, "a sandwich made with Italian bread that's usually toasted." But that definition really doesn't do the panini justice. A panini is more than a toasted sandwich—much more. Something wonderful happens when you use the two metal cooking plates of a panini press to heat up meats, cheeses, vegetables, and anything else you can think of between two slices of crispy and chewy bread. If you look at all the pieces of a panini, on paper or in the dictionary, it may seem like a toasted sandwich—but in reality it is much more than the sum of its parts.

What Is a Panini?

A panini is a hot sandwich that is cooked on a panini press so that the ingredients are heated and the flavors are blended together. The meats and cheeses become a gooey delight. The vegetables and sauces have their flavors locked inside the bread. And the bread becomes nice and crispy. If you're tired of making boring sandwiches for lunch every day, then it's time to get yourself a panini press.

The word *panino* is the Italian word for sandwich. Panini is actually the plural form of the word. The confusion is probably caused by the fact that you make panini in a panini press. In the United States and Canada it's perfectly acceptable to call one hot pressed sandwich a panini.

FACT

If you were in Italy and went up to a sandwich man to place your order, you'd probably ask for *un panino al prosciutto*. And if you were ordering for you and a friend, you might order *due* (two) *panini*. Asking for *due panini* when you're by yourself is also fine if you have a hearty appetite.

There are thousands of different panini recipes, and each of them can have many variations. The number of combinations and possibilities are almost endless, but the majority of panini recipes follow a simple formula. Take two slices of delicious crusty bread, add a serving of meat, a serving of cheese, and some sort of spread, and then cook it in a panini press. If you can do that, then you're on your way to some fantastic panini meals.

Great Ingredients, Great Panini

If you want to make great-tasting panini, you need great ingredients. There's nothing wrong with having a grilled cheese panini on white bread every once in a while, but when you're looking for a really satisfying meal you should go the extra mile and use the best ingredients possible. Take a trip to a gourmet market or a specialty cheese shop and pick up a few items. When you do, that plain grilled cheese panini could become a four cheese panini made with Asiago, Havarti, Brie, and Cheddar cheeses. And forget about that white bread because you could use ciabatta bread that's still warm from your baker's oven.

Using panini ingredients that are right out of your vegetable garden, or just baked, or straight from your butcher, aren't always necessary. But if it's in your budget or if you have the time and you want a gourmet-tasting panini, then you may want to go upscale for the following ingredients.

Fresh Mozzarella

The shredded mozzarella that comes in a bag at the supermarket will do just fine for everyday panini, but for special occasions you must try fresh mozzarella. You can buy a ball of fresh mozzarella at a good Italian deli. Don't worry if you aren't going to use the entire ball of cheese. You can store it in a container with water and a splash of milk. Be sure to fill the container with enough water to cover the mozzarella, and then add some milk.

Cold Cuts

Buying prepackaged cold cuts probably isn't a great idea. If you plan on making great panini, then you should get to know your butcher—or at least the guy behind the deli counter.

Homemade Sauces and Condiments

Making a homemade sauce or condiment can turn average ingredients into something special. But don't go out of your way to make a single serving of something like pesto or olive tapenade just for one panini. Make a big batch and keep it in your fridge so that you can enjoy it on a bunch of panini throughout the week.

Fresh Fruits and Vegetables

Using fresh produce is an important part of making a great panini. To prove this, all you need to do is go to your local farmer's market in July and pick up tomatoes and melon. Once you taste the difference you'll want to sue your supermarket for false advertising. The difference is really that dramatic. Gardening is becoming a popular hobby lately; get out there and grow some vegetables for your panini. Of course, you'll have to make do with what you have throughout the winter, but when you can you should always use fresh produce.

Fresh Seafood

If you're lucky enough to have a local fish market nearby, you should take advantage of it. Fresh fish will always taste better than frozen. Although lately, with gourmet markets like Trader Joe's, the quality of frozen seafood is improving.

Butcher Cuts of Meat

Getting to know your butcher to ensure that you get the freshest cuts of meat used to be a way of life, but in today's impersonal supermarkets you're lucky if you even see the same person behind the meat counter twice. Here's a secret for you: The items that are on sale are most likely over-stocked. There's nothing special about that item—it's just that they want to sell their supply before it spoils or goes bad.

When you buy your meats, you should also plan for leftovers. Buy a roast beef, get it a little bigger than you normally would, and use the rest for a panini the next day. You probably already do this on Thanksgiving because you enjoy turkey sandwiches, so why not do it more than once a year? If you're buying filet mignon for a get-together, get a couple extra steaks and cook them all together. If you have what you need for a delicious panini already in your fridge, you're going to have a lot more panini.

Choosing the Right Bread

Bread can make or break a panini. The difference between a loaf of white bread from the supermarket and an artisanal loaf from a gourmet bakery is huge, and the difference that it will make tastewise on your panini is even bigger. Selecting the right bread can turn a so-so sandwich into a party in your tummy.

Find a good bakery near you and start going regularly. Talk to the people behind the counter and find out what their baking schedule is like. Do they make all the same breads every day, or do you need to know which day to come to get a special loaf of bread? Perhaps on Thursdays they make a Kalamata olive bread, or on Sunday they make a jalapeño corn bread. If you've been going there every Monday, you may be missing out.

When you get that bakery schedule down, buy what you need plus some extra to freeze until your next visit. Place the bread in sealable plastic bags and they will last for weeks. Frozen bread doesn't lose much of its taste and texture when defrosted.

ESSENTIAL

When defrosting frozen bread, leave it in the plastic bag and let it thaw for a few hours. If you're in a rush, you can put the bread in the oven on very low heat, but that will toast the bread and change its flavor a little bit.

Here is a list of some varieties of bread you should try to make your panini with:

- Rustic, crunchy **Italian bread** can be used in almost any panini recipe, even the dessert panini.
- **Challah bread** is made with lots of eggs. It's a traditional Jewish bread which has significance in many Jewish holidays. It will also have significance in many of your panini.
- **Rye bread** is made with the flour from rye grain. It's darker and denser than regular breads and has a stronger flavor.
- Many of the French toast panini recipes in this book can be made with **cinnamon raisin bread** with great results. Dessert panini made with fruits and jams are also a good match for this sweet bread.
- **Pumpernickel bread** is similar to rye bread because it's made from rye grains, but bakers also add molasses, coffee, or cocoa powder to give it that signature brown color.
- **Sourdough bread** is made without added yeast. Instead you make a "starter" from wild yeast, which you feed with flour and water. This starter can be kept alive in your fridge for years if you keep it well-fed. Each time you make sourdough bread you add some starter and then

you feed and store the remaining starter. Sounds like a science experiment gone wrong, but it's really delicious bread.

- **Ciabatta bread** took the world by storm in the 1990s. You couldn't go to a sandwich shop without hearing someone ordering it, and you probably also heard it mispronounced. The correct way to say it is "cha-batta." It's soft and chewy on the inside, and it has a thin, crunchy, rustic crust which is delicious by itself, and is even better when used to make a panini.
- **Whole-grain bread** is much healthier than bread made with regular flour. If you're looking to slim down or just eat better, try some of the many different kinds of whole-grain breads.
- A **honey oat bread** is perfectly suited for anything from a peanut butter and jelly panini to a cocktail party panini.
- **Focaccia** is a flat, oven-baked bread that is usually topped with herbs or other ingredients. A focaccia panini is a treat because it's like eating a sandwich on an everything bagel. Popular focaccia breads can be baked with herbs, cheeses, or even vegetables. A roasted pepper and garlic focaccia is good enough to eat by itself.
- Getting a good **bagel** is sometimes a little easier than getting a good loaf of Italian bread. If that's the case in your neighborhood, then be sure to use bagels for hearty panini sandwiches. Just remember that any cheese or topping that's placed over the bagel hole will ooze out onto your panini press. Put a slice of meat or salad green leaf over the hole to keep the ingredients where they belong, inside the panini.
- **Peasant round Italian bread** is usually baked in a wood-fired oven, and its crust has a crisp, charred taste, while the inside remains spongy and chewy. Your best bet to find a peasant round Italian bread is to locate a farmers' market with an Amish bakery stand.

Baking Your Own Bread

If you don't have a bakery nearby or you are tired of buying the same bread varieties over and over, you should look into baking your own bread. The bread maker has become a popular appliance, and it takes all the fuss out of bread baking.

Baking bread from scratch is a big commitment. Not many people have a wood-fired oven in their homes anymore. But using a bread machine is a huge timesaver. Also, many different kinds of rustic European breads can be easily made by using the bread maker to create the dough and then a pizza stone to cook it in a regular oven.

Buying a Panini Press

If you've never seen a panini press before, it could be described as a cross between a waffle iron and a grill. There are two metal grill plates on a hinge. The plates are the source of the heat and are also used to press the panini together. Ridges in the metal grill plates give a cooked panini its signature grill marks.

If you're looking to purchase a panini press in a store or online, it would be a good idea to know some of the aliases that it can be sold as. You might see it marketed as a panini maker, a panini grill, a sandwich press, or even an indoor grill. What it's called isn't as important as the features that it includes. Here are some of the things to consider when buying a panini press.

How It Looks

If may sound like a superficial concern, but looks are actually pretty important. If your panini press is buried in a cabinet or put into storage because it's not stylish enough for your counter, you are never going to make any panini. The panini press needs to be on the counter, ready to indulge all of your hot sandwich needs at a moment's notice. Since you're going to be looking at it every day, it needs to look good.

FACT

A classic stainless steel panini press looks great in most kitchens. But don't worry if you have a retro kitchen with all red appliances— manufacturers also offer many color and style choices.

Nonstick Surface

If a panini press is too hard to clean, you will never want to use it. No one likes cleaning up a huge mess, so look for a press with nonstick cooking plates. Even better would be detachable, dishwasher-safe cooking plates. It's no fun making an awesome belly-busting panini and then having to spend an hour scraping your grill. That time should be spent on the sofa in a peaceful food coma. Make sure that the grill plates are nonstick. Cleaning up after making a panini shouldn't take longer than eating the panini. Easy cleanup is a huge plus.

Floating Hinge

A floating hinge helps adjust the position of the cooking plates to fit even the really thick panini sandwiches. So whether it's a one-inch T-bone steak or a tiny baloney and cheese on white bread, the grill plates will be in the best position to cook it exactly how you like it.

Temperature Settings

More control of the temperature means more control of your sandwiches. Look for a panini press with a slider that controls the temperature.

Drip Spout

Another great feature that's available is a drip spout in the grill plates. This comes in handy when you're cooking something really greasy like a hamburger. You can just put a small container or sometimes even a coffee cup next to the drip spout to catch the greasy runoff. Some panini presses will even include a cup or tray to catch the grease.

Reversible Cooking Plates

Some panini presses come with reversible cooking plates. One side of the plate has the usual ridges that you're used to seeing on a panini press. The other side is flat like a griddle and perfect for cooking pancakes or eggs, which can be used in some of the recipes in this book.

Safety Features

Another important thing to consider when picking out a sandwich maker is safety. The Krups panini maker has a cool-touch handle. This is handy because no one wants to get a potholder when making a sandwich.

Choosing a good panini grill with all the cool features over a bargain basement model is a sure way to ensure that it becomes a permanent fixture on your kitchen counter. And it's a lot easier to make a panini if you don't have to pull the panini press out of the closet first.

But even if you don't have a panini grill, you can also make panini in a frying pan or on a grill with a weight on it. The weight is important because pressing the ingredients together helps them heat up quickly. You can even make a panini with a George Foreman Grill.

Panini Press Tips and Tricks

Here are some panini press tips and tricks to get help you get the most out of your panini press.

Who says that you are limited to only making panini on a panini press? The panini press is basically an indoor grill and should be used as such. You can cook steaks, chicken breast, seafood, shish kebabs, and more. And if your panini press has reversible cooking plates or a griddle attachment, then bring on the omelets and pancakes too. No, you are not limited to cooking just panini, and in this book there are recipes that will show you how to cook wontons, French toast, grilled vegetables, and even a Cornish game hen.

ESSENTIAL

You need to know the limits of your bread. If you're using a thin slice of bread, don't overload it with spreads or sauces.

Use the panini press to cook as much of the meal as you can. There's no need to cook onions and the hamburgers on the stove and then move everything to the panini grill for the final press. You can fry up your onions and also cook the hamburger patties directly on your panini grill. It is a grill, after all. If the panini calls for bacon, cook the bacon on the press.

Don't worry about the timing it takes to keep everything warm. You don't have to worry about cooking everything at once like you would usually do to ensure that nothing gets cold before you serve it. When you cook panini style, everything heats up during the final press, so you don't have to worry about timing. For example, if the recipe calls for onions and peppers, cook them first and put them aside. You can even chop up double or triple the amount that the recipe calls for and then store the excess in the fridge for another day. The final press will ensure that everything is warm.

Grilling hamburgers or fatty meats will create a lot of grease. You may need to wipe down the panini press before moving on to the next step of the recipe. But remember to always be careful when handling a hot grill. A big wad of damp paper towels held in your hand while you're wearing an oven mitt is a good way to safely wipe down your grill.

Clean your panini press well after you use it. There's nothing worse than getting all the ingredients together to make a dessert panini and then pre-heating the panini press and smelling the last thing you cooked with it. You may be able to get away with it if the last thing you made was another dessert panini, but if it was something like salmon or marinated shish kebab, you're out of luck.

ALERT

Cleaning a panini press is a little bit dangerous if you're not careful. To avoid burns, you should always wear an oven mitt when cleaning your panini press. Do it near the sink and use a little water on a sponge or paper towels to wash away the grease and the stuff that oozes out of the panini. Never submerge your panini press. Electricity and water do not mix!

When you are piling ingredients on the bread, stay clear of the edges. In order to avoid a big mess when things ooze out of the sides, you need a good seal. Keeping the ingredients away from the edges of the bread will do just that. Recipes that include jelly or sauces can be very messy, but if you get a good seal, then you'll lock them inside the bread where they belong.

The size and thickness of the bread will determine how much sauce or other wet ingredients you can add. Thinly sliced bread will cause the panini to fall apart while cooking, and if that happens, it will be a nightmare to clean up. If you want to make something like a chili panini, you really need to break out the big crusty bread and cut it thick. Dryer panini can be made with thinly sliced bread so that you can appreciate the flavors of the ingredients more. There's a fine line between a soggy panini mess and moist, delicious panini.

Create a pocket in the bread for your fillings. This will keep the ingredients inside the panini while it presses, and it also gives you something to snack on while you're waiting for the panini to cook.

Let your panini cool before wrapping it up in aluminum foil, or else it will steam itself into a soggy mess. If you can get ahold of butcher's paper, use that instead of foil. If the hot panini is able to release that heat, it won't turn to mush.

QUESTION

How can I incorporate panini into my everyday routine?
Make your panini when you have time and freeze them. This way you can just grab something out of the freezer before heading out to work or school in the morning. By lunchtime your panini will be thawed. And if you let the sandwich cool before wrapping it up, it should still stay crispy. A minute in the microwave will give you results that are acceptably close to fresh off the panini press.

When making grilled cheese panini, put any additional ingredients in between the cheese. Put a layer of cheese on the bread, then the other ingredients (meats, pesto, salsa, etc.), and then another layer of cheese. This not only helps glue the panini together but also gives you a nice flavor surprise in the center of your sandwich.

Experimentation Is the Key to Panini Success

There are many keys to making a great-tasting panini sandwich. The thickness of the bread is important, as is the ratio of cold cuts to sauces to vegetables. You'll need to experiment for a while before you get the hang of it. Make a lot of panini and it will become second nature. And making a lot of panini will be a lot of fun.

If you try a recipe from this book and it didn't suit your palate, then think about how to improve it. What would make your next panini better?

Think about it and then try it. What do you have to lose? Even a bad panini is still pretty tasty.

And don't worry if you can't find the exact ingredients that appear in this book. Feel free to leave things out or add completely different ingredients because that's all that you have on hand. A panini should not be an expensive meal—unless you want it to be. Leftovers from dinner the night before will make some of the most delicious panini. You wouldn't make a tray of eggplant Parmesan just for a panini, but there's nothing stopping you from using those leftovers to make a fantastic panini. You may even start planning your dinners with the leftovers in mind so that you can use them to make panini.

Get creative in the kitchen. If you have an idea for a panini or an interesting way to use your panini press, what's stopping you from trying it? Get your ingredients together and start experimenting. What's the worst that can happen? You make something that doesn't taste good? There's not too much at risk here, but you could be rewarded with a delicious new meal that no one has thought of before.

When experimenting with your panini press, it's good to have an open mind and use your imagination. You can make panini as simple or elaborate as you wish. If you can cook it with heat, then you can probably cook it with your panini press. Good luck.

CHAPTER 2

Breakfast Panini

Ham, Egg, and Cheese Panini

This popular breakfast sandwich is even better as a panini. To recreate that breakfast shop taste, use American cheese and a round roll.

INGREDIENTS | **SERVES 1**

3 slices ham
2 eggs
1 hard Kaiser roll
2 tablespoons butter
2 slices American cheese
1 slice lettuce
2 slices tomato
1 tablespoon ketchup (optional)

1. Preheat the panini press. Cook ham slices on hot panini press for 1–2 minutes and set aside.

2. In a small frying pan coated with nonstick cooking spray, crack and fry 2 eggs and set aside.

3. Slice roll open and spread butter onto both sides.

4. Put ham, cheese, fried eggs, lettuce, tomato, and optional ketchup on roll bottom, and cover with roll top. Place on panini press. Close lid and cook for 3–4 minutes.

5. Remove from press and slice in half. Serve warm.

Corn Bread, Bacon, and Tomato Panini

Lots of people put bacon in their corn bread. If you're making it from scratch, you may want to give it a try.

INGREDIENTS | **SERVES 1**

2 strips bacon
2 slices corn bread
3 tomato slices

1. Preheat the panini press. Cook bacon in the heated panini press and place on paper towel–lined plate to absorb grease.

2. Place bacon on 1 slice of corn bread.

3. Add tomato slices on top of bacon and close sandwich.

4. Place on panini press, close lid, and cook for 3–5 minutes.

5. Remove from press, slice in half, and serve warm.

¼ cup chopped onions
¼ cup chopped green bell peppers
¼ cup diced ham
Nonstick spray, as needed
3 eggs
2 slices whole wheat bread
¼ cup shredded Cheddar cheese

Western Cheddar Omelet Panini

Why have an omelet with toast on the side when you can have it all together in a panini?

1. Preheat the panini press. Add onions, peppers, and ham to a hot frying pan that's been coated with cooking spray. Crack eggs into a bowl and beat until yolks and whites are mixed. Pour eggs into frying pan over the other ingredients. Cook for 2–4 minutes, then carefully flip. Cook for an additional 2–4 minutes.

2. Remove omelet from pan and place on 1 slice of bread. You may have to cut the omelet to get it to fit on the bread. Add the cheese, close the sandwich, and place it on the panini press.

3. Close lid and cook for 2–4 minutes or until cheese is melted and bread is golden brown.

4. Remove from panini press, cut in half, and serve warm.

The Omelet Panini

Making your favorite omelet panini style is easy. Since this omelet is going into a panini press, there's no need for perfection. You can even make it like scrambled eggs and mix the eggs up in the pan while cooking. Just make your eggs and put them in your panini press between two slices of bread. You can also add additional cheeses if you like.

INGREDIENTS | SERVES 1

2 tablespoons olive oil
½ cup spinach
2 eggs
2 slices rye bread
¼ cup grated Swiss cheese

Spinach and Swiss Omelet on Rye

Swiss cheese on eggs is always a popular choice. With the deep flavor of rye bread, this panini makes for a filling breakfast or brunch.

1. Preheat the panini press. Add olive oil and spinach to a hot frying pan and sauté for a few minutes. If using frozen spinach, be sure to strain as much water as you can from the spinach to avoid splatter. Crack eggs into a bowl and beat until yolks and whites are mixed. Pour eggs into frying pan over the spinach and cook for 2–4 minutes. Carefully flip and cook for an additional 2–4 minutes.

2. Remove omelet from pan and place on 1 slice of rye bread. You may have to cut the omelet to best fit on the bread. Add the cheese, close the sandwich, and place it on the panini press.

3. Close lid and cook for 2–4 minutes or until cheese is melted and bread is golden brown.

4. Remove from panini press, cut in half, and serve warm.

Breakfast Quesadilla

Quesadillas are popular appetizers at Mexican restaurants, but you can also make them panini style at breakfast time.

1. On a preheated panini press, cook 2 breakfast sausages, following instructions on the package, and set aside.

2. Crack two eggs in a bowl and beat until a smooth consistency is achieved. Add to a heated frying pan that has been coated with cooking spray. Scramble eggs and set aside.

3. Chop sausage, and spread over half of the tortilla. Add eggs to the same side of the tortilla and sprinkle Cheddar cheese on top. Fold tortilla in half.

4. Place folded tortilla on panini press, close lid, and cook for 3–5 minutes.

5. Remove from panini press and slice into four triangles. Serve with Salsa (see Chapter 19) and sour cream, if desired.

Cold Ingredients

Often, panini recipes will instruct you to cook an ingredient and then set it aside. You may also find yourself using leftovers from the refrigerator as ingredients. There's no reason to worry about cold ingredients because the panini press will reheat everything.

INGREDIENTS | SERVES 2

½ cup butter

2 egg yolks

1 teaspoon lemon juice

Pinch salt

Pinch cayenne pepper (optional)

2 eggs

2 slices Canadian bacon

2 English muffins

Eggs Benedict Panini

No need to poach these eggs. Hollandaise sauce makes fried eggs taste fantastic.

1. In a double boiler over medium heat, melt the butter. Add the egg yolks and whisk constantly. Do not let the eggs cook or curdle. Lower heat if necessary. Add lemon juice, salt, and a sprinkle of cayenne pepper, if desired. Mix well, remove from burner, and set aside.

2. Preheat the panini press. In a frying pan coated with nonstick cooking spray, fry 2 eggs until the yolks are set. Over easy eggs will be too runny in the panini press and ooze out of the sandwich.

3. Fry Canadian bacon on panini press and set aside.

4. Fork split the English muffins and place bottoms on panini press. Add Canadian bacon and eggs, then drizzle a few tablespoons of hollandaise sauce on top. Top English muffins and close panini press.

5. Cook 2–4 minutes. Serve immediately.

Seafood Eggs Benedict

Many restaurants add crabmeat or salmon to Eggs Benedict, and you can too. While assembling the panini, add smoked salmon or crabmeat before the hollandaise sauce. Who says you can't have a fancy brunch in the comfort of your own home?

Breakfast Pigs in a Panini

Nothing beats pancakes and sausage for a hearty breakfast, except maybe pancakes and sausage grilled in a panini press.

1. Cook sausage following the instructions on the package, and slice them in half lengthwise. Preheat the panini press.

2. Place sliced sausage on top of 2 pancakes and drizzle maple syrup on top of sausage. Top sandwiches with 2 more pancakes and place on panini press. Close lid and cook for 2–4 minutes.

3. Remove from panini press, slice in half, and serve with maple syrup for dunking.

Rolling Your Panini

Breakfast pigs in blankets are often served rolled up in a tube shape. In order to recreate that shape with your panini press, you'll need some toothpicks to hold it all together. After rolling the pancakes around the sausage, poke one or two toothpicks into the side to keep it from unrolling. The panini press will seal the pig in the blanket, so be sure to remove the toothpicks before serving.

INGREDIENTS | SERVES 2

2 strips bacon

2 eggs

4 cooked pancakes (use your favorite recipe or pancake mix)

½ cup maple syrup plus extra for dunking

Bacon, Egg, and Pancake Panini

Why should you have to make the tough choice of eggs or pancakes for breakfast when you can have both? Throw in bacon or sausage into this panini and you won't have to eat again until lunchtime.

1. Preheat the panini press. Cook bacon in the heated panini press for 2–4 minutes, then place on paper towel–lined plate to absorb grease.

2. Cook eggs any way you like. Both fried or scrambled go well in this panini.

3. Place eggs on top of 2 pancakes and top with bacon. Pour ½ cup maple syrup over the bacon and top with remaining pancakes. Place on panini press and cook for 2–4 minutes.

4. Remove from panini press, cut it in half, and serve with maple syrup for dunking.

1 garlic or everything bagel
2 tablespoons cream cheese
4 slices smoked salmon
1 slice red onion

Scoop Your Bagel

Scooping out the innards of a bagel is usually done to cut down on calories, but it will also give you more room for the salmon and cream cheese in this recipe.

Smoked Salmon and Cream Cheese Panini

Putting a bagel in a panini press will give it a crispy and delicious crust that's perfect for enjoying with smoked salmon and cream cheese.

1. Preheat the panini press. Cut open a bagel and spread cream cheese on one side. Add the smoked salmon and the onion slices to the other side, and place cream cheese side on top.

2. Place it on the panini press, close lid, and cook for 2–4 minutes.

3. Remove and cut in half. Serve warm.

¼ cup blueberries
2 slices corn bread
2 tablespoons honey

Blueberries

Blueberries are not only delicious but they are also low in calories and loaded with antioxidants. Their tangy flavor tastes great in everything from pies to panini.

Corn Bread and Blueberry Panini

If you're looking for a sweet and savory panini, add your favorite fruit to some corn bread. Blueberries add a fruity kick to corn bread that can't be beat.

1. Preheat panini press. Arrange blueberries on 1 slice of corn bread and drizzle with honey.

2. Top panini with another slice of corn bread.

3. Place on panini press, close lid, and cook for 3–5 minutes.

4. Remove from press, slice in half, and serve.

INGREDIENTS | SERVES 1

3 slices mozzarella cheese (or ⅓ cup shredded cheese)
2 slices corn bread

Mozzarella Corn Bread Panini

You may have enjoyed something similar to this recipe at a carnival or a fair. They're really easy to make at home too. This recipe makes a great lunch served with a hot bowl of soup.

1. Preheat panini press to medium heat setting.

2. Place mozzarella cheese on 1 slice of corn bread.

3. Top panini with another slice of corn bread.

4. Place on panini press, close lid, and cook for 3–5 minutes.

5. Remove from press, slice in half, and serve.

Arepa

Arepa is a popular Columbian dish made from unleavened cornmeal that's formed into a round patty and grilled like a pancake. It is usually stuffed with cheese, meat, eggs, or seafood. Many arepa recipes can be made with a panini press using corn bread or corn pancakes as a substitute. Or if you can find arepa corn meal in a store near you, why not try making them from scratch? The taste will be worth the effort.

1 egg
½ cup milk
1 teaspoon cinnamon
2 slices bread

French Toast

French toast made in a panini press comes out crispier than traditional French toast.

1. Preheat the panini press. In a flat bowl or any other container that will fit 1 slice of bread, add egg, milk, and cinnamon. Mix well with a whisk.

2. Dunk bread slices into mixture one at a time, coating both sides.

3. Place soaked bread slices on panini press and close lid.

4. Cook for 4–5 minutes or until desired crispness is achieved.

5. Remove from press and serve immediately with maple syrup and butter.

Cinnamon

Cinnamon is a spice made from the inner bark of several species of trees in the Cinnamomum genus. The curled shape of cinnamon sticks is how the bark dries after it's stripped from the tree.

1 egg

½ cup milk

3 teaspoons cinnamon, divided

1 apple, peeled and chopped

3 tablespoons butter

2 teaspoons sugar

2 slices cinnamon raisin bread

Powdered sugar, to taste

Dairy-Free and Vegan French Toast

You can make French toast with a few minor substitutions. Swap out the milk with soymilk or almond milk, and for the butter you can use a vegetable-oil-based butter replacement product such as Earth Balance. If you don't eat eggs, then a ripe mashed banana can be used instead.

Cinnamon Raisin French Toast with Apples

French toast on a panini press is a winning combination. But stuffed French toast is even better. This recipe is like having apple pie with your French toast. You almost don't need the maple syrup.

1. Preheat the panini press. In a large flat container, mix egg, milk, and 1 teaspoon cinnamon with a whisk and set aside.

2. Place apple in a small frying pan over medium heat. Add butter, 2 teaspoons cinnamon, and sugar, and cook for about 4 minutes, stirring constantly.

3. Place 1 slice of bread on a plate and add a heaping portion of apple mixture to the center of the bread. Try to leave some room near the edges of the bread to avoid leakage while the panini is being pressed. Top with second slice of bread and dunk the entire sandwich into the milk mixture. No need to soak the bread—just a quick dip will do. Carefully flip it over to coat both sides of the sandwich without losing any of the filling. There's no neat way to do this, so you will want the preheated panini press nearby to minimize any dripping mess on your kitchen floor.

4. Place coated sandwich on panini press and close lid. Cook for 3–5 minutes.

5. Remove from press and slice panini in half. Dust with powdered sugar and serve maple syrup for dunking.

INGREDIENTS | SERVES 1

1 egg

½ cup milk

1 teaspoon cinnamon

2 slices Challah bread

⅓ cup fresh blueberries

Powdered sugar and whipped cream, to taste

Challah French Toast Stuffed with Fresh Blueberries

Challah bread is an egg bread that is traditionally eaten on Jewish holidays. It has a soft texture and an eggy flavor that makes wonderful French toast.

1. Preheat the panini press. In a large flat container, mix egg, milk, and cinnamon with a whisk.

2. Place 1 slice of bread on counter and add the blueberries. Top the panini with the second slice of bread and dunk into milk mixture.

3. Flip sandwich over and coat other side with milk mixture.

4. Place coated sandwich on panini press and close lid. Cook for 3–5 minutes.

5. Remove from press and slice panini in half. Dust with powdered sugar and a dollop of whipped cream, if desired.

1 egg
½ cup milk
1 teaspoon cinnamon
2 slices honey oat bread
⅓ cup fresh sliced strawberries
Powdered sugar, to taste

Honey Oat French Toast with Fresh Strawberries

With all the combinations of bread and fresh fruit out there, you could eat French toast almost every day and never feel like you're having the same thing twice.

1. Preheat the panini press. In a large flat container, mix egg, milk, and cinnamon with a whisk.

2. Place 1 slice of bread on counter and add the strawberries. Top the panini with the second slice of bread and dunk into milk mixture.

3. Flip sandwich over and coat other side with milk mixture.

4. Place the coated sandwich on the panini press and close lid. Cook for 3–5 minutes.

5. Remove from press and slice panini in half. Dust with powdered sugar and serve with maple syrup.

Strawberries

There are over 600 varieties of strawberries that differ in size and flavor. June bearing strawberries are productive in June, while everbearing strawberries are ready to harvest in the spring and then again in the fall.

INGREDIENTS | SERVES 1

1 egg
½ cup milk
1 teaspoon cinnamon
2 slices honey oat bread
3 tablespoons blackberry jam
Powdered sugar, to taste

Stuffed French Toast with Blackberry Jam

If you don't have fresh fruit on hand, you can always use jams and jellies to stuff your French toast.

1. Preheat the panini press. In a large flat container, mix egg, milk, and cinnamon with a whisk.

2. Place 1 slice of bread on counter and spread with the blackberry jam. Keep the jam away from the edges of the bread to avoid oozing. Top the panini with the second slice of bread and dunk into milk mixture.

3. Flip sandwich over and coat other side with milk mixture.

4. Place coated sandwich on the panini press and close lid. Cook for 3–5 minutes.

5. Remove from press and slice panini in half. Dust with powdered sugar and serve with maple syrup.

Invasive Blackberries

In places like New Zealand and Australia, blackberries are considered an invasive species. Goats are sometimes used to help stop these serious weeds from spreading.

1 egg

½ cup milk

1 teaspoon cinnamon

2 slices Challah bread

4 tablespoons peanut butter

⅛ cup chocolate chips

Powdered sugar, to taste

Peanut Butter and Chocolate Stuffed French Toast

This peanut butter and chocolate panini is a decadent way to start your day. You will probably want to clear your morning schedule, because you may find yourself taking a nap after this rich panini.

1. Preheat the panini press. In a large flat container, mix egg, milk, and cinnamon with a whisk.

2. Place 1 slice of bread on counter and spread with peanut butter.

3. Add chocolate chips on top of peanut butter. Top the panini with the second slice of bread and dunk into milk mixture.

4. Flip sandwich over and coat other side with milk mixture. Place coated sandwich on panini press and close lid. Cook for 3–5 minutes.

5. Remove from press and slice panini in half. Dust with powdered sugar and serve with a dollop of whipped cream and/or maple syrup.

Peanut Butter Chips

Peanut butter chips will work well in this recipe too. Use the same amount of peanut butter chips as you do chocolate chips. Use even more if you want the peanut butter flavor to dominate.

2 links breakfast sausage

1 egg

½ cup milk

1 teaspoon cinnamon

2 slices honey oat bread

Sausage Stuffed French Toast

No time to sit down and enjoy a hearty French toast and sausage breakfast? Take it on the go! With the help of your panini press, this messy breakfast becomes an on-the-go meal that you can eat with your hands.

1. Cook breakfast sausage according to instructions on the package and set aside. Slice links in half lengthwise.

2. Preheat the panini press. In a large flat container, mix egg, milk, and cinnamon with a whisk.

3. Place 1 slice of bread on counter and add sliced sausage links. Top the panini with the second slice of bread and dunk into milk mixture. Flip sandwich over and coat other side with milk mixture.

4. Place coated sandwich on panini press and close lid. Cook for 3–5 minutes.

5. Remove from press and slice panini in half. Serve with a cup of maple syrup for dunking.

1 egg

½ cup milk

1 teaspoon cinnamon

2 slices Portuguese sweet bread

3 tablespoons orange marmalade

3 tablespoons cream cheese

Powdered sugar, to taste

Orange Marmalade Stuffed French Toast

You'll enjoy this recipe if you've already tried several of the fruit-filled French toasts and are ready to take it to the next level. The addition of cream cheese makes this stuffed French toast taste more like a Danish pastry. Whether it's breakfast time, snack time, or tea time, this panini will do the trick.

1. Preheat the panini press. In a large flat container, mix egg, milk, and cinnamon with a whisk.

2. Place 1 slice of bread on counter and spread with the orange marmalade. Spread cream cheese on the second slice of bread and place onto other half. Dunk sandwich into milk mixture, then flip to coat opposite side.

3. Place coated sandwich on panini press and close lid. Cook for 3–5 minutes.

4. Remove from press and slice panini in half. Dust with powdered sugar and serve with a dollop of whipped cream, if desired.

Portuguese Sweet Bread

Portuguese sweet bread is bread made with the addition of milk and sugar or honey. It's sweet and has a light texture, and is perfect for French toast.

1 egg
½ cup milk
1 teaspoon cinnamon
2 slices Challah bread
¼ cup fresh blueberries
2 tablespoons chopped pecans
Powdered sugar, to taste

Pecan and Blueberry Stuffed French Toast

There are so many different ways to make French toast that you could eat it every day and never tire of it.

1. Preheat the panini press. In a large flat container, mix egg, milk, and cinnamon with a whisk.

2. Place 1 slice of bread on counter and add blueberries. Sprinkle chopped pecans on top of blueberries. Top the panini with the second slice of bread and dunk into milk mixture. Flip sandwich over and coat other side with milk mixture.

3. Place coated sandwich on panini press and close lid.

4. Cook for 3–5 minutes.

5. Remove from press and slice panini in half. Dust with powdered sugar and serve with maple syrup.

French Toast Sticks

If serving this recipe at a brunch you may want to try making French toast sticks. All you have to do is cut the panini into strips after you dunk it in the French toast mixture. It'll be messy but worth it.

INGREDIENTS | **SERVES 1**

3 slices Taylor ham
1 egg
1 hard roll
2 slices American cheese

Taylor Ham, Egg, and Cheese Panini

A favorite Jersey shore breakfast sandwich that is even better as a panini. Perfect for the morning after a night out on the town.

1. Preheat the panini press. Place Taylor ham slices on panini press and cook for 3–5 minutes. Set aside.

2. In a nonstick spray-coated frying pan, scramble or fry an egg and set aside.

3. Cut open a hard roll and add the Taylor ham, the egg, and the cheese.

4. Place on panini press, close lid, and cook for 2–4 minutes.

5. Remove from press, cut in half, and serve warm.

Taylor Ham

Taylor ham is also known as pork roll. It's a pork-based meat product that comes in slices and can usually be found in delis and breakfast shops in the New Jersey and Philadelphia areas.

CHAPTER 3

Pressed Deli Sandwiches

Roast Beef, Bacon, and Cheddar Panini

This all-American sandwich seems the perfect lunch for the rugged guys who appear in beer commercials, but its taste will appeal to people of all shapes and sizes. A sourdough roll or crunchy Italian bread will be needed to hold the two servings of meat in this panini.

1. Preheat the panini press. Cook bacon on the panini press until crisp and set aside. Wearing an oven mitt, wipe bacon grease from panini press with a wad of paper towels.

2. Place 1 slice of bread or bottom half of roll on counter and spread with half the mayonnaise. Layer roast beef, bacon, and cheese on the bread.

3. Spread remaining mayonnaise onto second slice of bread or top half of roll and close the sandwich.

4. Place on panini press, close lid, and cook for 4–6 minutes.

5. Remove from press, cut in half, and serve warm.

A Homemade Pizza Peel for Panini

Use a cutting board or a plate to make the panini and then slide it onto your hot panini grill, much like pizza makers use a peel to slide their pizzas in and out of the oven.

Roast Beef and Provolone Panini

Roast beef isn't just for the meat and potatoes crowd. You can make some fancy roast beef panini with the addition of the right ingredients; in this case provolone cheese, arugula, and horseradish mayonnaise. You'll want a big crunchy roll for this panini.

1. Preheat the panini press. Place 1 slice of bread or bottom half of roll on counter.

2. Layer sliced roast beef on bread. Sprinkle with salt and pepper, and then add provolone cheese and arugula.

3. Spread horseradish mayonnaise onto top half of roll or bread and close the sandwich.

4. Place on panini press, close lid, and cook for 3–5 minutes.

5. Remove from press, cut in half, and serve warm.

Provolone

Provolone goes great with fruity white wines, antipasto, and of course, panini. High quality provolone is good enough to eat alone as a snack.

1 tablespoon olive oil
1 small yellow onion, sliced
¼ cup sliced mushrooms
1 teaspoon garlic powder
Salt and pepper, to taste
1 long roll or baguette
⅛–¼ pound roast beef

Roast Beef with Caramelized Onion Panini

A long roll or a baguette is the right bread for this panini.

1. Preheat the panini press. In a bowl add olive oil, onion, mushrooms, garlic powder, salt, and pepper and mix to coat the ingredients with the oil. Empty bowl onto heated panini press and drizzle additional olive oil on top as desired. Cook for 4–5 minutes. After 3 minutes, you may open panini press and mix ingredients with a wooden spoon to ensure that they are evenly cooked. Remove from panini press and set aside.

2. Place bottom half of roll or baguette on counter and add sliced roast beef on bread. Sprinkle with salt and pepper and top with onion mixture.

3. Add top of roll or baguette and place sandwich on panini press.

4. Close panini press and cook for 3–5 minutes.

5. Remove panini, slice in half, and serve warm.

1 seeded Kaiser or Portuguese roll
⅛–¼ pound oven-roasted turkey
2 slices provolone cheese
3 tomato slices
1 tablespoon mayonnaise
Salt and pepper, to taste

Turkey and Provolone Panini

The key to this panini recipe is to use quality ingredients. You need to find an upscale market or a great deli that sells oven-roasted turkey, or cook one yourself. And find a cheese shop that will sell you a chunk of premium provolone instead of the slices that you find at your supermarket.

1. Preheat the panini press. Cut your roll and place bottom half on work surface. Lay slices of turkey on bottom half of roll and then add provolone cheese. Arrange tomato slices on top of cheese.

2. Spread mayonnaise onto the other side of roll and add salt and pepper.

3. Close sandwich and place on heated panini press.

4. Cook for 3–5 minutes, and then remove from press.

5. Cut panini in half, and serve with a pickle if desired.

Kaiser Roll

A Kaiser roll can sometimes be called a hard roll or a Vienna roll. It's a crusty round roll and can also be made with a topping of sesame or poppy seeds.

⅛ pound oven-roasted turkey, sliced

2 thick slices bread

2 slices Muenster cheese

½ small avocado, peeled and sliced

2 red onion slices

2 thinly cut roasted red pepper strips

Salt and pepper, to taste

1 tablespoon mayonnaise

Turkey Avocado Panini

There are lots of wet ingredients in this panini, so you'll want a thickly sliced Italian bread or an equivalent substitution. Pumpernickel bread and rye are also good options.

1. Preheat the panini press. Lay slices of turkey on 1 slice of bread and add Muenster cheese. Add avocado on top of cheese. If the avocado keeps falling apart, that's a good thing. That means that it's very ripe, so scoop it onto the sandwich with a spoon if you have to.

2. Add onion and roasted red pepper. You don't want too much red pepper because there are already lots of wet ingredients in this sandwich. Add just enough to get some flavor. Sprinkle salt and pepper to taste.

3. Spread mayonnaise onto remaining slice of bread.

4. Top sandwich, place on panini press, and close the lid. Cook for 3–5 minutes.

5. Remove from panini press and cut in half. Serve warm.

Storing Avocado

Once an avocado is cut it will turn brown pretty quickly. To store the leftover avocado for a few days, drizzle some lemon juice on it and put it in a sealed plastic bag with the air removed.

Salami and Provolone Panini

INGREDIENTS | SERVES 1

4–6 slices Genoa salami
2–4 slices provolone cheese
2 slices Italian bread

Panini to Go

If you're taking a panini to go, let it cool before wrapping in aluminum foil or a sandwich bag. If you wrap it too soon, the hot sandwich will get soggy. A crisp and dry panini can be reheated in a microwave oven with good results.

If you make a panini to bring with you for lunch every day, you might not have time to break out the cutting board and make a complicated panini before you leave for work or school. You'll need some recipes that are quick and easy to make but still taste delicious. This salami and provolone panini will meet your needs.

1. Preheat the panini press. Add slices of salami and cheese to 1 slice of bread. Then top with additional slice of bread.

2. Place on panini press and close lid. Cook for 3–5 minutes.

3. Remove from panini press, slice in half, and serve warm.

Salami, Mozzarella, and Artichoke Panini

INGREDIENTS | SERVES 1

4–6 slices salami
⅛ cup shredded mozzarella
1 ciabatta roll
2 or 3 artichoke hearts, chopped

Good quality salami from an Italian deli makes supermarket salami look like baloney.

1. Preheat the panini press. Add salami and cheese to bottom half of roll.

2. Add artichoke hearts to sandwich.

3. Close sandwich with top of roll.

4. Place on panini press, close lid, and cook for 3–5 minutes.

5. Remove from panini press, slice in half, and serve warm.

2 slices Italian bread or roll

3 slices ham

3 slices Genoa salami

3 slices pepperoni

2 slices mozzarella cheese

⅛ cup sliced roasted red peppers

2 slices tomato

2 tablespoons oil and vinegar dressing

Italian Combo Panini

The Italian Combo is one of the most popular sandwiches in delis, even though it's made a little differently in each one. Be sure to try many different variations of this panini. You won't be disappointed.

1. Preheat the panini press. If using Italian bread, cut to desired length and then slice lengthwise.

2. Add ham, salami, pepperoni, and mozzarella cheese to 1 slice of bread. Top meat with the roasted red peppers and tomato slices.

3. Drizzle oil and vinegar dressing on other slice of bread and top sandwich. Use enough dressing to flavor the bread without soaking it, or else your panini will fall apart.

4. Place on panini press, close lid, and cook 4–6 minutes.

5. Remove from press and cut in half. Serve warm.

Popular Variations

Choose your favorites from the following popular Italian Combo ingredients: capicola ham, mortadella, pepperoni, salami, dried sausage, mozzarella cheese, provolone cheese, sweet peppers, black olives, onion, lettuce, tomato, balsamic vinegar, Italian dressing.

3 strips bacon

2 tablespoons mayonnaise

2 slices sourdough bread

2 slices tomato

¼ cup shredded lettuce

B.L.T. Panini

In case you don't know, B.L.T. is an abbreviation for bacon, lettuce, and tomato. The traditional way to make a B.L.T. is to cook the bacon and toast separately and then add the cold ingredients. When you make a B.L.T. panini style, you heat up all the ingredients together for a familiar yet unique taste.

1. Preheat the panini press. Cook bacon on the heated panini press until crisp and set aside.

2. Wearing an oven mitt, wipe panini press with a wad of paper towels to remove excess grease.

3. Spread mayonnaise on both slices of bread and add bacon, tomato, and shredded lettuce to one side of sandwich. Then top sandwich with the second slice of bread.

4. Place on panini press and cook 3–5 minutes.

5. Remove from press, cut in half, and serve with a pickle, if desired.

Variations

You can add cheese, avocado, or even ranch dressing to this panini if you are looking for some variety.

3 strips bacon

2 tablespoons mayonnaise

2 slices whole wheat bread

2–3 slices oven-roasted turkey, sliced

¼ cup shredded lettuce

2 slices tomato

Turkey Club Panini

Just like the B.L.T., the turkey club panini takes on a familiar yet unique taste when it's heated in a panini press.

1. Preheat the panini press. Cook bacon on the panini press until crisp and set aside.

2. Wearing an oven mitt, wipe panini press with a wad of paper towels to remove excess grease.

3. Spread mayonnaise on both slices of bread and add bacon to one side of sandwich. Next lay the turkey, lettuce, and tomato. Then top sandwich with the second slice of bread.

4. Place on panini press, close lid, and cook 3–5 minutes.

5. Remove from press, cut in half, and serve with a pickle, if desired.

Cuban Sandwich

INGREDIENTS | SERVES 1

1 Kaiser roll
3 slices ham
3 slices roasted pork
2 slices Swiss cheese
1 sliced pickle
1 tablespoon mustard

Traditional Cuban sandwiches are made in a press called a plancha, which has no grooves on the cooking surface. Grooves or no grooves, either way is delicious.

1. Preheat the panini press. Cut the roll in half and layer ham, roasted pork, and Swiss cheese on the bottom half.

2. Add pickle slices to sandwich. Spread the mustard onto the top of the roll and place on top of sandwich.

3. Place on panini press, close lid, and cook for 3–5 minutes.

4. Remove from press, cut in half, and serve warm.

Reuben Panini

INGREDIENTS | SERVES 1

5 slices pastrami
2 slices Swiss cheese
2 slices rye bread
¼ cup sauerkraut
2 tablespoons Russian dressing

You could also make this panini with corned beef. Pumpernickel bread is another option that you should try.

1. Preheat the panini press. Pile the pastrami and Swiss cheese onto 1 slice of bread. Top with sauerkraut, and then spread the Russian dressing on the other piece of rye bread before placing on top of the sauerkraut.

2. Place on panini press, close lid, and cook for 3–5 minutes.

3. Remove from press, cut in half, and serve warm.

4 slices roast beef

3 slices smoked Gouda cheese

2 slices sourdough bread

1 tablespoon Garlic Mayonnaise (see Chapter 19)

Roast Beef and Gouda on Sourdough

Sourdough bread has a unique tangy taste that is a nice match with roast beef and Gouda cheese.

1. Preheat the panini press. Lay the roast beef and Gouda cheese on 1 slice of sourdough bread.

2. Spread the Garlic Mayonnaise on the other slice of bread and close the sandwich.

3. Place on panini press, close lid, and cook for 3–5 minutes.

4. Remove from press, cut in half, and serve warm.

Variation

French bread or a baguette can be used for this recipe if you have no sourdough bread on hand. Cut the loaf into sandwich-sized pieces, 4–8 inches, and slice lengthwise. The insides of the bread can be scooped out to fit more roast beef and cheese if desired.

5 slices pastrami
1 sliced sour pickle
2 slices marbled rye bread
1 tablespoon mustard

Pastrami on Rye

This is a classic deli sandwich that usually consists of pastrami stacked a few inches high. Save that extra pastrami for a second sandwich when making it in a panini press. You don't want your panini to topple over.

1. Preheat the panini press. Place the pastrami and the sliced pickle on 1 slice of bread.

2. Spread the mustard on the other slice of bread and close the sandwich.

3. Place on panini press, close lid, and cook for 3–5 minutes.

4. Remove from press, cut in half, and serve warm.

Marbled Rye

The most popular variety of marbled rye is made with traditional rye dough and pumpernickel dough. It is a dense and very filling bread.

Pastrami and Coleslaw Panini

Coleslaw keeps this panini from getting too dry, but you may need some thicker slices of bread to keep it all under wraps.

1. Preheat the panini press. Pile the pastrami, Swiss cheese, and sliced pickle onto 1 slice of bread. Top with coleslaw, and then spread the horseradish on the other piece of rye bread.

2. Place on panini press, close lid, and cook for 3–5 minutes.

3. Remove from press, cut in half, and serve warm.

Coleslaw on a Panini

When adding toppings such as coleslaw on a panini, you have the potential to make a big mess on your panini press. Adjust the amount of coleslaw to fit the limitations of the bread. You'll want enough to keep the panini moist, but not too much, or else the bread will get soggy and fall apart.

Ham, Turkey, and Gouda Panini

INGREDIENTS | SERVES 1

3 slices roasted turkey

3 slices ham

2 slices Gouda cheese

2 slices rye bread

2 slices tomato

½ teaspoon horseradish

1 tablespoon mayonnaise

Rye bread is always good with ham and turkey. Garlic Mayonnaise (see Chapter 19) would be a nice addition as well.

1. Preheat the panini press. Pile the roasted turkey, ham, and Gouda cheese onto 1 slice of bread. Top with tomato, and then spread the horseradish and mayonnaise on the other slice of bread.

2. Place on panini press, close lid, and cook for 3–5 minutes.

3. Remove from press, cut in half, and serve warm.

Cheese Steak with the Works

INGREDIENTS | SERVES 1

2 tablespoons olive oil

1 teaspoon minced garlic

3 slices onion

3 slices bell pepper

¼ cup sliced mushrooms

1 hoagie roll

3–5 thin slices cooked steak

4 slices Cheddar cheese

There's a place for those frozen steak slices that most cheese steak vendors use, but it's not in this panini. Use that leftover T-bone or filet mignon instead.

1. Preheat the panini press. In a bowl, combine the olive oil, garlic, onion, bell pepper, and mushrooms. Mix well until evenly coated with the oil. Pour onto a heated panini press and cook for 3–5 minutes. Remove and set aside.

2. Cut open the hoagie roll and add the steak, Cheddar cheese, and the cooked vegetables.

3. Place on the panini press and cook for another 2–4 minutes.

4. Cut in half and serve warm.

2 slices corn bread

3 slices ham

3 slices mozzarella cheese

Variations

You can spread butter over the corn bread before putting it on the panini press for a more tasty panini. Some people even put butter on the inside of the panini to keep the ham and cheese company. You can also try it with mayonnaise.

Ham and Cheese on Corn Bread

Can't find corn bread at your bakery? Make a batch of corn muffins in a bread pan instead.

1. Preheat the panini press. On 1 slice of corn bread, arrange slices of ham and mozzarella cheese, and top with another slice of bread.

2. Place on the panini press and close the lid.

3. Cook for 3–5 minutes. Remove from press and slice in half. Serve warm.

1 croissant

3 slices ham

3 slices Cheddar cheese

Variation

A croissant is high in calories and contains a good deal of fat. To make a healthier version of this recipe, replace the croissant with whole grain bread or a whole wheat English muffin.

Ham and Cheese Croissant

How do you jazz up a ham and cheese sandwich? You put it on a croissant and press it in your panini maker.

1. Preheat the panini press. Cut open croissant and add the ham and the cheese.

2. Place on panini press, close lid, and cook for 3–5 minutes.

3. Remove from press, cut in half, and serve warm.

3 slices ham

3 slices salami

5 slices pepperoni

3 slices provolone cheese

2 slices Italian bread

Ham, Salami, Pepperoni, and Provolone Panini

These Italian cold cuts stack really nicely. Pile them up at least a quarter of an inch high. Don't worry, the cheese will hold it all together.

1. Preheat the panini press. Lay ham, salami, pepperoni, and provolone cheese on 1 slice of bread.

2. Top with another slice of bread and place on panini press.

3. Close lid and cook for about 2–4 minutes.

4. Cut in half and serve warm.

Variation

Pesto mayonnaise makes a great addition to this panini. Combine 3 tablespoons Pesto Sauce (see Chapter 19) with a cup of mayonnaise and blend well in a food processor. It can be stored in the refrigerator for up to a week.

4 slices pineapple

2 slices Italian bread

3 slices ham

Grilled Pineapple and Ham Panini

Grilled pineapple has such as great flavor that you really don't need the ham or the bread in this panini. It's great as a snack by itself!

1. Preheat the panini press. Add the pineapple slices to the panini press and cook for 2–4 minutes. Set aside.

2. On 1 slice of bread, add the ham and the pineapple slices. Top sandwich with another slice of bread.

3. Place on panini press, close lid, and cook for 3–5 minutes.

4. Remove from press, cut in half, and serve warm.

CHAPTER 4

Burgers

Cheeseburger Panini Style

No need to fire up the barbecue for these burgers. You can cook the burger on your panini grill, then put the burger on a roll or hearty bread with cheese and press it again. They should add panini-style burgers to fast-food menus!

1. Preheat the panini press. Place hamburger patty on the heated panini press. If your press has a drip spout for excess grease to run off, you'll want to put a small container underneath.

2. Cook 3–4 minutes, less if a rare burger is desired. Remove cooked burger and set aside.

3. Wearing an oven mitt, wipe burger grease from panini press with a wad of paper towels.

4. Put burger inside the hamburger roll and top with cheese. Place back on panini press and cook for an additional 1–2 minutes.

5. Remove from press and serve with a side of ketchup and a pickle.

Hamburger Buns

There are many varieties of buns and breads that can be used for hamburger panini. Besides regular hamburger buns you could also use a Kaiser roll or Italian bread sliced about ⅓ inch thick. Brioche buns are made with more eggs and butter than regular bread and also complement a burger well.

1 hamburger patty
1 hamburger roll
2 slices mozzarella cheese
2 tablespoons tomato sauce

Pizza Burger Panini

The most popular fast-food restaurants usually serve burgers or pizza. Why not combine both of these favorites using your panini press?

1. Preheat the panini press. Place hamburger patty on panini press. If your press has a drip spout for excess grease to run off, you'll want to put a small container underneath.

2. Cook 3–4 minutes, less if a rare burger is desired. Remove cooked burger and set aside.

3. Wearing an oven mitt, wipe burger grease from panini press with a wad of paper towels.

4. Put burger inside the hamburger roll and top with cheese and tomato sauce. Place back on panini press and cook for an additional 1–2 minutes.

5. Remove from press and serve with small bowl of tomato sauce for dunking.

Pizza Burger Panini Variations

To spice up your pizza burger panini, add pepperoni, sausage, mushroom, or your favorite pizza topping.

INGREDIENTS | SERVES 1

1 small yellow onion, sliced
1 hamburger patty
2 slices rye bread
2 slices Swiss cheese

Patty Melt

No need to go to a diner for these patty melts. Using your panini press to grill the onions and burger will recreate that diner taste right in your own home. Rye bread is the traditional way to make a patty melt, but sourdough works great too.

1. Preheat the panini press and spray with nonstick cooking spray. Place onion slices on panini press. Grill onions for 2–4 minutes and set aside.

2. Place hamburger patty on panini press. If your press has a drip spout for excess grease to run off, you'll want to put a small container underneath. Cook 3–4 minutes, less if a rare burger is desired. Remove cooked burger and set aside.

3. Wearing an oven mitt, wipe burger grease from panini press with a wad of paper towels.

4. Place the hamburger patty on 1 slice of bread. Top with Swiss cheese and grilled onions. Top with the other slice of bread and place on panini press. Cook 2–4 minutes.

5. Cut in half and serve with a small bowl of ketchup or mustard for dipping.

1 hamburger patty
1 hamburger roll
⅓ cup feta cheese
¼ cup chopped fresh spinach leaves

Spinach Feta Burger

How can you make a burger more healthy? Add a leafy green vegetable to it. Spinach gets the job done in this recipe.

1. Preheat the panini press. Place hamburger patty on panini press. If your press has a drip spout for excess grease to run off, you'll want to put a small container underneath.

2. Cook 3–4 minutes, less if a rare burger is desired. Remove cooked burger and set aside.

3. Wearing an oven mitt, wipe burger grease from panini press with a wad of paper towels.

4. Put burger inside the hamburger roll and top with feta cheese and spinach. Place back on panini press and cook for an additional 1–2 minutes.

5. Remove from press and serve hot.

Spinach Feta Burger Variations

Cook the spinach with olive oil and garlic before adding to the burger.

INGREDIENTS | SERVES 1

1 hamburger patty

1 hamburger roll

3 slices Monterey jack cheese

2 tablespoons Poblano Chili Sauce (see Chapter 19)

Poblano Chili Burger

Poblano pepper sauce takes a regular hamburger and turns it into a gourmet burger. Some Monterey jack cheese will cool off the slight heat from the peppers without changing the smoky flavor.

1. Preheat the panini press. Place hamburger patty on panini press. If your press has a drip spout for excess grease to run off, you'll want to put a small container underneath.

2. Cook 3–4 minutes, less if a rare burger is desired. Remove cooked burger and set aside.

3. Wearing an oven mitt, wipe burger grease from panini press with a wad of paper towels.

4. Put burger inside the hamburger roll and top with Monterey jack cheese. Add a generous helping of Poblano Chili Sauce. Place back on panini press and cook for an additional 1–2 minutes.

5. Remove from press and serve hot.

Poblano Versus Ancho

Poblano peppers are smoky and about as hot as a jalapeño pepper. When they are smoked and dried they become ancho peppers.

Veggie Burger Panini

INGREDIENTS | SERVES 1

1 veggie burger patty
1 hamburger roll
1 avocado, sliced
3 slices tomato

Bread or a Roll?

You can enjoy any of the panini burger recipes in this book with thick slices of bread instead of a roll. They become more like a patty melt than a burger. Why not try a rye or pumpernickel panini burger too?

If you've sworn off red meat but still have burger cravings, you're probably a big fan of veggie burgers. And with a panini press you can squeeze even more vegetables into the roll.

1. Preheat the panini press. Place veggie burger patty on panini press and cook for 3–4 minutes.

2. Put burger inside the hamburger roll and top with sliced avocado and tomato.

3. Place back on panini press and cook for an additional 1–2 minutes.

4. Remove from press and serve hot.

Barbecue Salmon Burger

INGREDIENTS | SERVES 1

1 salmon burger
1 whole-grain roll
2 tablespoons barbecue sauce
2 slices red onion

Barbecue Salmon Burger Variation

If you marinate the salmon burger in the barbecue sauce for at least an hour, it will absorb even more of the sauce's flavor. The burger will also be much juicier.

Just because salmon comes from the sea doesn't mean that you can't slather it with good old-fashioned barbecue sauce.

1. Preheat the panini press. Cook salmon burger on panini press for 4–5 minutes. Remove from press and place on a roll. Add the barbecue sauce and the onion slices.

2. Place top of roll on the burger to close the sandwich, and put the burger on the panini press. Close the lid.

3. Cook for 2–3 minutes. Remove from press and slice in half. Serve warm.

2 tablespoons olive oil
½ onion, sliced
¼ cup mushrooms, sliced
1 teaspoon garlic powder
Salt and pepper, to taste
1 hamburger patty
1 hamburger roll
3 slices Swiss cheese

Mushroom Swiss Burger

Mushroom and Swiss cheese burgers will usually require extra napkins. Using two thick slices of chewy bread instead of a hamburger roll keeps the mess to a minimum.

1. Preheat the panini press. In a bowl add olive oil, onion, mushrooms, garlic powder, salt, and pepper and mix to coat the ingredients with the oil. Empty bowl onto preheated panini press and drizzle additional olive oil on top if desired. Cook for 4–5 minutes. After 3 minutes you may open panini press and mix ingredients with a wooden spoon to ensure that they are more evenly cooked. Remove from panini press and set aside.

2. Place hamburger patty on panini press. If your press has a drip spout for excess grease to run off, you'll want to put a small container underneath. Cook 3–4 minutes, less if a rare burger is desired. Remove cooked burger and set aside.

3. Wearing an oven mitt, wipe burger grease from panini press with a wad of paper towels.

4. Put burger inside the hamburger roll and top with Swiss cheese and grilled mushrooms and onions. Close the burger with the top of the roll and place it back on the panini press to cook for an additional 1–2 minutes.

5. Remove from press and serve hot.

INGREDIENTS | **SERVES 1**

4 frozen onion rings
1 hamburger patty
1 hamburger roll
3 tablespoons barbecue sauce
4–6 pickle slices

Barbecue Burger

Adding barbecue sauce to a burger has a dramatic effect on the flavor. Use your panini press to seal that flavor in the roll along with some pickles and fried onion rings. Be sure to have extra napkins on hand.

1. Preheat the panini press. Place frozen onion rings on panini press and close lid. Cook for 3–5 minutes, depending on size of onion rings. Remove from panini press and set aside.

2. Place hamburger patty on panini press. If your press has a drip spout for excess grease to run off, you'll want to put a small container underneath. Cook 3–4 minutes, less if a rare burger is desired. Remove cooked burger and set aside.

3. Wearing an oven mitt, wipe burger grease from panini press with a wad of paper towels.

4. Put burger inside the hamburger roll and top with barbecue sauce. Add pickles, onion rings, and top of bun, then place it back on panini press and cook for an additional 1–2 minutes.

5. Remove from press and serve hot.

INGREDIENTS | **SERVES 1**

3 strips bacon

1 hamburger patty

1 hamburger roll

¼ cup crumbled blue cheese

Bacon Blue Cheese Burger

The key to this burger is getting a good quality blue cheese. If you can't find one, blue cheese dressing will make an acceptable substitution. There's a big difference between the two, but both will make for a great burger.

1. Preheat the panini press. Place bacon strips on panini press and cook until crisp. Remove and set aside.

2. Place hamburger patty on panini press. If your press has a drip spout for excess grease to run off, you'll want to put a small container underneath. Cook 3–4 minutes, less if a rare burger is desired. Remove cooked burger and set aside.

3. Wearing an oven mitt, wipe burger and bacon grease from panini press with a wad of paper towels.

4. Put burger inside the hamburger roll and top with bacon strips and blue cheese. Close roll and place it back on panini press to cook for an additional 1–2 minutes.

5. Remove from press and serve hot.

Types of Bacon

There are a few varieties of bacon that you should consider if you're looking for an interesting variation of this recipe. Besides regular bacon, you should also try it with Canadian bacon, applewood-smoked bacon, or even pancetta.

Onion Burger

There's nothing but onions on this burger, so you may want to save this recipe for when you make homemade burger patties to really enjoy the flavor of the ground beef.

1. Preheat the panini press. Place onion on panini press. Grill for 2–4 minutes and set aside.

2. Place hamburger patty on panini press. If your press has a drip spout for excess grease to run off, you'll want to put a small container underneath. Cook 3–4 minutes, less if a rare burger is desired. Remove cooked burger and set aside.

3. Wearing an oven mitt, wipe grease from panini press with a wad of paper towels.

4. Put burger inside the onion roll and top with grilled onions. Spread Garlic Mayonnaise on the other side of the roll. Close roll and place it back on panini press to cook for an additional 1–2 minutes.

5. Remove from press and serve hot.

INGREDIENTS | SERVES 1

1 hamburger patty

1 Kaiser roll

3 slices pepper jack cheese

2 tablespoons Guacamole (see Chapter 19)

1 tablespoon Salsa (see Chapter 19)

2 teaspoons Chipotle Mayonnaise (see Chapter 19)

Santa Fe Burger Panini

You'll need a big roll to keep all the toppings in this one, or just serve it with a fork to scoop up anything that falls out. You won't want to waste it.

1. Preheat the panini press. Place hamburger patty on panini press. If your press has a drip spout for excess grease to run off, you'll want to put a small container underneath. Cook 3–4 minutes, less if a rare burger is desired. Remove cooked burger and set aside.

2. Wearing an oven mitt, wipe grease from panini press with a wad of paper towels.

3. Put burger inside the roll and top with pepper jack cheese, Guacamole, and Salsa. Spread Chipotle Mayonnaise on the other side of the roll and close burger. Place it back on panini press to cook for an additional 1–2 minutes.

4. Remove from press and serve hot.

Ham, Egg, and Burger Panini

Using the roll to soak up the egg yolk is the best part of this burger.

1. Preheat the panini press. In a small frying pan coated with nonstick cooking spray, crack and fry an egg and set aside.

2. Place hamburger patty on panini press. If your press has a drip spout for excess grease to run off, you'll want to put a small container underneath. Cook 3–4 minutes, less if a rare burger is desired. Remove cooked burger and set aside.

3. Wearing an oven mitt, wipe grease from panini press with a wad of paper towels.

4. Put burger inside the hamburger roll and lay the fried egg on top. Next add the ham, cheese, and onion, and then close the burger. Place it back on panini press to cook for an additional 1–2 minutes.

5. Remove from press and serve hot.

Hamburger Patties

To ensure that your homemade hamburger patties cook evenly, pinch the centers of the burgers so that the edges are just a little bit thicker than the center. This way the thicker edges that have more surface area will cook at the same rate as the thinner center.

1 salmon burger patty
2 thick slices Italian bread
1 small onion, sliced
2 slices tomato
¼ cup shredded lettuce
1 tablespoon tartar sauce

Salmon Burger

A burger from the sea for the health-conscious panini maker. Leave the roll in the bread box for this one and go with thick bread slices from a round loaf of Italian bread.

1. Preheat the panini press. Place salmon burger patty on panini press. Cook for 2–3 minutes. Remove cooked salmon burger and set aside.

2. Wearing an oven mitt, wipe grease from panini press with a wad of paper towels.

3. Place salmon burger on 1 slice of bread and add onion, tomato, and lettuce. Spread the tartar sauce on the second slice of bread and close the burger. Place it back on panini press to cook for an additional 1–2 minutes.

4. Remove from press and serve hot.

Salmon Burgers

Salmon burgers can contain up to 10 grams of fat less than traditional burgers. It's a great choice if you're watching your fat intake or just love salmon.

INGREDIENTS | SERVES 1

3 slices bacon
2 slices pineapple
1 hamburger patty
1 hamburger roll
1 tablespoon ranch dressing

Ranch Burger

Canadian bacon would be a nice addition to this burger.

1. Preheat the panini press. Place bacon strips and pineapple slices onto panini press and cook until bacon is crisp and pineapple is charred. Remove and set aside.

2. Place hamburger patty on panini press. If your press has a drip spout for excess grease to run off, you'll want to put a small container underneath. Cook 3–4 minutes, less if a rare burger is desired. Remove cooked burger and set aside.

3. Wearing an oven mitt, wipe burger and bacon grease from panini press with a wad of paper towels.

4. Put burger inside the hamburger roll and lay bacon on top. Next add the pineapple and ranch dressing, and close the burger. Place it back on panini press to cook for an additional 1–2 minutes.

5. Remove from press and serve hot.

1 hamburger patty
1 Kaiser roll
¼ cup chili
1 small onion, chopped
3 slices Cheddar cheese

Texas Chili Burger

Two words: big roll. You'll need it to soak up all the chili and cheese. Put out loads of napkins too.

1. Preheat the panini press. Place hamburger patty on panini press. If your press has a drip spout for excess grease to run off, you'll want to put a small container underneath. Cook 3–4 minutes, less if a rare burger is desired. Remove cooked burger and set aside.

2. Wearing an oven mitt, wipe grease from panini press with a wad of paper towels.

3. Put burger inside the roll and spoon chili on top. Next, add the onion and Cheddar cheese and close the burger. Place it back on panini press to cook for an additional 1–2 minutes.

4. Remove from press and serve hot.

1 hamburger patty

1 hamburger roll

2 tablespoons Olive Tapenade (see Chapter 19)

¼ cup crumbled feta cheese

2 green pepper slices

Greek Burger

If you make your own tapenade, use Kalamata olives for this one.

1. Preheat the panini press. Place hamburger patty on panini press. If your press has a drip spout for excess grease to run off, you'll want to put a small container underneath. Cook 3–4 minutes, less if a rare burger is desired. Remove cooked burger and set aside.

2. Wearing an oven mitt, wipe burger grease from panini press with a wad of paper towels.

3. Put burger inside the hamburger roll and spoon the Olive Tapenade on top. Next, add the crumbled feta cheese and the green pepper slices. Close the burger and place it back on panini press to cook for an additional 1–2 minutes.

4. Remove from press and serve hot.

INGREDIENTS | **SERVES 1**

1 hamburger patty
1 hamburger roll
3 slices Cheddar cheese
5 slices jalapeño pepper
1 tablespoon Salsa (see Chapter 19)

Nacho Burger

Mixing an envelope of taco seasonings in with a pound of ground beef will make this burger much better. If using store-bought burgers, then rub some on top before cooking.

1. Preheat the panini press. Place hamburger patty on panini press. If your press has a drip spout for excess grease to run off, you'll want to put a small container underneath. Cook 3–4 minutes, less if a rare burger is desired. Remove cooked burger and set aside.

2. Wearing an oven mitt, wipe burger grease from panini press with a wad of paper towels.

3. Put burger inside the hamburger roll and add the Cheddar cheese. Next, add the jalapeño peppers and the Salsa. Close the burger and place it back on panini press to cook for an additional 1–2 minutes.

4. Remove from press and serve hot with extra Salsa for dunking.

Variations

Roasted jalapeño peppers go great on a burger. Just place the peppers in the panini grill and cook them until they're blackened. Remove from the grill, scrape off all the char marks, and discard. Cut off the stems and remove the seeds, and your roasted peppers are ready for your burger.

1 hamburger patty

1 hamburger roll

2 tablespoons Pesto Sauce (see Chapter 19)

5 slices sun-dried tomatoes

3 slices mozzarella cheese

Pesto Burger

If making homemade burger patties, add some extra pesto in with the ground beef for additional flavor.

1. Preheat the panini press. Place hamburger patty on panini press. If your press has a drip spout for excess grease to run off, you'll want to put a small container underneath. Cook 3–4 minutes, less if a rare burger is desired. Remove cooked burger and set aside.

2. Wearing an oven mitt, wipe burger grease from panini press with a wad of paper towels.

3. Put burger inside the hamburger roll and spoon the Pesto Sauce on top. Next, add the sun-dried tomatoes and mozzarella cheese. Close the burger and place it back on panini press to cook for an additional 1–2 minutes.

4. Remove from press and serve hot with an additional dab of Pesto Sauce for dunking.

1 chicken breast

½ cup buffalo wing sauce, plus more to taste

Salt and pepper, to taste

1 Kaiser roll

1 tablespoon blue cheese dressing

Buffalo Chicken Burger

The hot sauce marinade for the chicken breast is the way to go.

1. Marinate chicken breast in buffalo wing sauce for at least an hour.

2. Preheat the panini press. Place chicken breast on panini press, and discard sauce used for marinade. Sprinkle with salt and pepper before closing lid. Cook for 4–6 minutes, depending on thickness of the chicken breast. Remove from panini press and set aside.

3. Wearing an oven mitt, wipe grease and sauce from panini press with a wad of paper towels.

4. Put chicken inside the roll and add fresh buffalo wing sauce. Next, add the blue cheese dressing. Close the roll and place it back on panini press to cook for an additional 1–2 minutes.

5. Remove from press and serve hot with additional blue cheese dressing for dunking.

1 salmon burger patty
3 pineapple rings
1 Kaiser roll
3 tablespoons teriyaki sauce

Teriyaki Salmon Burger

Teriyaki and pineapple go together like peas and carrots. If you really like teriyaki flavor, then let the salmon and pineapple marinate in separate bowls of sauce for a while before grilling them. It'll make a big mess on your panini press, but it's worth it.

1. Preheat the panini press. Place salmon burger on panini press and close lid. Cook for 1–2 minutes then add pineapple rings. Cook another 2–3 minutes. Remove from press and place on a roll. Add the teriyaki sauce.

2. Place the burger into the panini press and close the lid.

3. Cook for 2–3 minutes. Remove from press and slice in half. Serve warm.

1 portobello mushroom cap
2 tablespoons olive oil
1 teaspoon garlic powder
1 whole-grain roll
3 slices mozzarella cheese
3 slices roasted red peppers
2 tablespoons Pesto Sauce (see Chapter 19)

Portobello Pesto Burger

A portobello mushroom is a perfectly acceptable substitute for a hamburger.

1. Preheat the panini press. Place portobello mushroom cap on panini press. Drizzle with olive oil and sprinkle with garlic powder. Close lid and cook for 2–4 minutes.

2. Remove mushroom from press and place on a roll. Add the mozzarella cheese and roasted red peppers. Spread the Pesto Sauce on the lid of the roll and place on top of sandwich.

3. Place on the panini press and close the lid.

4. Cook for 2–3 minutes. Remove from press and slice in half. Serve warm.

1 hamburger patty

1 hamburger roll

3 slices provolone cheese

3 tablespoons Spinach Pesto (see Chapter 19)

2 leaves red leaf lettuce

2 slices tomato

¼ cup caramelized onions

Spinach Pesto Burger

If making the burger patties from scratch, add a few tablespoons of the Spinach Pesto in with the ground beef.

1. Preheat the panini press. Place hamburger patty on panini press and close the lid. If your press has a drip spout for excess grease to run off, you'll want to put a small container underneath.

2. Cook 3–4 minutes, less if a rare burger is desired. Remove cooked burger and set aside.

3. Wearing an oven mitt, wipe burger grease from panini press with a wad of paper towels.

4. Put burger inside the hamburger roll and top with cheese, Spinach Pesto, lettuce, tomato slices, and caramelized onions. Place back on panini press, close the lid, and cook for an additional 1–2 minutes.

5. Remove from press and cut in half. Serve warm.

1 hamburger patty
1 hamburger bun
¼ cup alfalfa sprouts
3 slices avocado
1 tablespoon honey Dijon mustard

Honey Dijon Burger

Alfalfa sprouts add a crisp flavor to any burger, and they're very nutritious.

1. Preheat the panini press. Place hamburger patty on panini press and close the lid. If your press has a drip spout for excess grease to run off, you'll want to put a small container underneath.

2. Cook 3–4 minutes, less if a rare burger is desired. Remove cooked burger and set aside.

3. Wearing an oven mitt, wipe burger grease from panini press with a wad of paper towels.

4. Put burger inside the hamburger roll and top with sprouts, avocado, and mustard. Place back on panini press, close the lid, and cook for an additional 1–2 minutes.

5. Remove from press and cut in half. Serve warm.

1 hamburger patty
1 hamburger bun
3 slices Brie cheese
⅛ cup sun-dried tomatoes
¼ cup chopped artichoke hearts

Brie Burger

Pat the sun-dried tomato and artichoke hearts with paper towels before putting them on this burger. It could get pretty messy if you don't.

1. Preheat the panini press. Place hamburger patty on panini press and close the lid. If your press has a drip spout for excess grease to run off, you'll want to put a small container underneath.

2. Cook 3–4 minutes, less if a rare burger is desired. Remove cooked burger and set aside.

3. Wearing an oven mitt, wipe burger grease from panini press with a wad of paper towels.

4. Put burger inside the hamburger roll and top with cheese, sun-dried tomatoes, and artichoke hearts. Place back on panini press, close the lid, and cook for an additional 1–2 minutes.

5. Remove from press and cut in half. Serve warm.

1 turkey burger patty
1 hamburger roll
3 tablespoons mango chutney
2 leaves red leaf lettuce
2 slices red onion

Mango Chutney Turkey Burger

Substitute a black bean burger or even a veggie burger if you're trying to avoid meat.

1. Preheat the panini press. Place burger patty on panini press and close the lid. If your press has a drip spout for excess grease to run off, you'll want to put a small container underneath.

2. Cook 5–6 minutes, less if a rare burger is desired. Remove cooked burger and set aside.

3. Wearing an oven mitt, wipe burger grease from panini press with a wad of paper towels.

4. Put burger inside the hamburger roll and top with mango chutney, lettuce, and onion slices. Close the burger. Place back on panini press, close the lid, and cook for an additional 1–2 minutes.

5. Remove from press and cut in half. Serve hot.

1 hamburger patty
½ red pepper, sliced
½ onion, sliced
¼ cup lime juice
2 tablespoons minced garlic
1 tablespoon cilantro
2 tablespoons olive oil
1 teaspoon cumin
1 hamburger roll,
1 tablespoon Salsa (see Chapter 19)
1 tablespoon sour cream

Fajita Burger

If making the hamburger patties yourself, mix a little lime juice in with the ground beef.

1. Preheat the panini press. Place hamburger patty on panini press and close the lid. If your press has a drip spout for excess grease to run off, you'll want to put a small container underneath. Cook 3–4 minutes, less if a rare burger is desired. Remove cooked burger and set aside.

2. Wearing an oven mitt, wipe burger grease from panini press with a wad of paper towels.

3. Place red pepper and onion in a bowl with the lime juice, garlic, cilantro, olive oil, and cumin. Mix well, then pour contents onto panini press. Cook for 3–5 minutes.

4. Put burger inside the hamburger roll and top with cooked pepper and onion slices, Salsa, and sour cream. Close sandwich. Place back on panini press, close the lid, and cook for an additional 1–2 minutes.

5. Remove from press and cut in half. Serve warm with additional sour cream and Salsa.

INGREDIENTS | SERVES 1

1 hamburger patty

1 Kaiser roll

2 slices Swiss cheese

3 slices ham

1 sliced pickle

2 tablespoons Garlic Mayonnaise (see Chapter 19)

Cuban Burger

A big Kaiser roll will be needed for this panini to keep all the ingredients from sliding out. A regular hamburger roll just won't cut it.

1. Preheat the panini press. Place hamburger patty on panini press and close the lid. If your press has a drip spout for excess grease to run off, you'll want to put a small container underneath.

2. Cook 3–4 minutes, less if a rare burger is desired. Remove cooked burger and set aside.

3. Wearing an oven mitt, wipe burger grease from panini press with a wad of paper towels.

4. Put burger inside the roll and top with Swiss cheese, ham, pickle slices, and Garlic Mayonnaise. Place back on panini press, close the lid, and cook for an additional 1–2 minutes.

5. Remove from press and cut in half. Serve warm.

Grilled Cheese

Basic Grilled Cheese

Making a grilled cheese on a panini press doesn't require gobs of butter like it does when you fry it. So try it if you're looking for a slightly healthier version.

1. Preheat panini press.

2. Add cheese to 1 slice of bread.

3. Close sandwich and place on panini press.

4. Close press, and heat for 3–5 minutes.

5. Remove and slice in half. Serve warm.

Monterey Jack and Jalapeño Pepper Panini

Monterey jack is a mild white cheese with a Mexican heritage even though it originated in Monterey, California. Adding to the Mexican theme are the jalapeño peppers and fresh tomatoes for a grilled cheese that tastes like it came from south of the border.

1. Preheat the panini press. Lay Monterey jack cheese slices on 1 slice of bread. Add jalapeño peppers and tomato slices.

2. Place the other slice of bread on top and place on the panini press.

3. Close lid and cook for 3–5 minutes.

4. Remove from press, cut in half, and serve warm.

2 slices ham

2 slices Italian bread

¼ cup shredded Cheddar cheese

1 apple, peeled and sliced

Apples

China is a the world's largest producer of apples. The United States ranks second, with the majority of U.S. apples coming from the state of Washington.

Ham, Cheddar, and Apple Panini

Some people put Cheddar cheese in their apple pies. Some people put apples in their cheese panini sandwiches. Either way, these ingredients taste great together.

1. Preheat the panini press. Lay slices of ham onto 1 slice of bread. Add the shredded cheese and the apple slices. Close the sandwich.

2. Place on panini press and close lid.

3. Cook for 3–5 minutes, and remove from press.

4. Slice in half and serve warm.

3 slices Swiss cheese

2 slices sourdough bread

2 teaspoons sliced jalapeño peppers

2 tablespoons Spinach Pesto (see Chapter 19)

Variation

To add a nice smoky flavor to this panini, replace the jalapeño pepper slices with chipotle peppers. If you need more heat try habanero peppers.

Swiss and Spinach Pesto Panini

Swiss cheese and leafy greens go well together. If you don't have spinach, try using arugula or radicchio.

1. Preheat the panini press. Lay Swiss cheese on 1 slice of bread. Add jalapeño peppers and then spoon the Spinach Pesto on.

2. Place the other slice of bread on top and place on panini press.

3. Close lid and cook for 3–5 minutes.

4. Remove from press, cut in half, and serve warm.

1 tablespoon olive oil
½ small yellow onion, sliced
¼ cup crimini mushrooms
1 teaspoon garlic powder
Salt and pepper, to taste
4 slices Gruyère cheese
1 ciabatta roll

Mushroom Gruyère Panini

A large ciabatta roll is great to soak up the flavors of this panini. If you don't have a roll then go with thick-sliced bread

1. Preheat the panini press. In a bowl add olive oil, onion, mushrooms, garlic powder, salt, and pepper and mix to coat the ingredients with the oil. Empty the bowl onto panini press and drizzle additional olive oil on top if desired. Close lid and cook for 4–5 minutes. After 3 minutes you may open panini press and mix ingredients with a wooden spoon to ensure that they are more evenly cooked. Remove from panini press and set aside.

2. Place Gruyère cheese on roll. Top with grilled onion and mushrooms.

3. Close roll and place on panini press.

4. Close lid and cook for 3–5 minutes and remove from press.

5. Cut in half and serve warm.

Variations
Swiss can be used as a less expensive substitute for Gruyère cheese.

2 slices bread

2 slices Asiago cheese

2 slices Havarti cheese

3 slices Brie cheese

2 slices Cheddar cheese

Variation

Why not add even more cheese flavor to this panini by using Asiago cheese bread? Cut it thick and give it a nice coat of butter before placing it on the panini press.

Four-Cheese Panini

This is the Cadillac of grilled cheese panini sandwiches. Asiago, Havarti, Brie, and Cheddar cheese cost more than American cheese slices, and after you taste this panini, you'll know why. You'll need a hearty, thickly sliced bread for all of this cheese.

1. Preheat panini press.

2. Arrange all the cheeses on 1 slice of bread.

3. Place another slice of bread on top and place on panini press.

4. Close lid and cook for 3–5 minutes.

5. Remove from press, cut in half, and serve warm.

4 slices bacon

4 slices Cheddar cheese

2 slices sourdough bread

3 slices tomato

Grilled Cheese with Bacon and Tomato

This standard diner fare is made even better with a panini press.

1. Preheat the panini press. Cook bacon on panini press until crisp.

2. Place the Cheddar cheese on top of 1 slice of bread. Then add the bacon and tomato. Top with the other slice of bread.

3. Place on panini press, close lid, and cook for 3–5 minutes.

4. Remove from press, cut in half, and serve warm.

2 slices Italian bread

2 tablespoons olive oil

⅓ cup feta cheese

¼ cup chopped Kalamata olives

2 slices onion

2 slices bell pepper

Grilled Feta with Kalamata Olives

This grilled cheese panini has a Greek flair to it. It's almost like a Greek salad panini.

1. Preheat the panini press. Drizzle the inside of both slices of bread with olive oil. Add feta cheese on top of 1 slice of bread.

2. Arrange Kalamata olives, onion, and bell pepper on top of feta cheese.

3. Top the sandwich with another slice of bread and place on panini press.

4. Close lid and cook for 3–5 minutes.

5. Remove from press, cut in half, and serve warm.

Chopping Olives

To chop olives you'll need a large cutting board because the olives will roll all over the place. Place the olives in a pile on the cutting board and using a slow chopping motion cut the olives into medium sized pieces. Or you can use a food processor with the pulse setting for a few seconds.

INGREDIENTS | SERVES 1

3 slices Swiss cheese
2 slices sourdough bread
½ avocado, peeled and sliced
2–3 artichoke hearts, chopped
1 teaspoon Dijon mustard

Dijon Grilled Swiss Cheese Panini

This grilled cheese is a treat for vegetable lovers. The Dijon mustard works well with the Swiss cheese for a unique-tasting grilled cheese panini.

1. Preheat the panini press. Add Swiss cheese on top of 1 slice of bread.

2. Lay the avocado slices on top of the Swiss cheese, then add the artichoke hearts on top of the avocado.

3. Spread Dijon mustard on the other slice of bread and close the sandwich.

4. Place on panini press, close lid, and cook for 3–5 minutes.

5. Remove from press, cut in half, and serve warm.

Avocado

The avocado is very nutritious and contains minerals such as iron, potassium, and calcium. They're not only good on panini but you can also make a facial mask with them. Mash 1 avocado with a teaspoon of honey. Drizzle with hot water until the desired consistency is achieved. Spread it over your face, avoiding nose and eyes, and leave on for 10 minutes before washing off.

Spicy Grilled Cheese

INGREDIENTS | SERVES 1

3 slices Monterey jack cheese
2 slices sourdough or corn bread
5 slices jalapeño pepper
1 tablespoon Salsa (see Chapter 19)

Variations

If you like it really spicy, then add some hot sauce or replace the jalapeño slices with roasted habanero peppers.

There are enough varieties of grilled cheese panini that you could eat them every day and not get bored.

1. Preheat the panini press. Place the Monterey jack cheese on top of 1 slice of bread.

2. Add the jalapeño pepper slices and spoon on the salsa. Add the other slice of bread on top.

3. Place on panini press, close lid, and cook for 3–5 minutes.

4. Remove from press, cut in half, and serve warm.

Grilled Cheese Taco Panini

INGREDIENTS | SERVES 1

½ cup ground beef
2 slices Monterey jack cheese
2 slices Cheddar jalapeño bread
2 slices Cheddar cheese
2 slices tomato
1 slice onion
1 tablespoon Salsa (see Chapter 19)
1 tablespoon sour cream

Variations

Add ¼ package of taco seasoning mix when browning the ground beef for a real taco flavor.

You can use a flour tortilla in place of bread for this grilled cheese.

1. Brown the ground beef in a preheated pan. Drain and set aside.

2. Preheat the panini press. Lay the Monterey jack cheese on 1 slice of bread. Add the Cheddar cheese, ground beef, tomato, onion, Salsa, and sour cream and cover with the other slice of bread.

3. Place on preheated panini press, close lid, and cook for 3–5 minutes.

4. Remove from press, cut in half, and serve warm.

Grilled Swiss Cheese with Sauerkraut Panini

Sauerkraut isn't just for hot dogs anymore. Try using stone-ground mustard to give this grilled cheese a nice bite.

1. Preheat the panini press. On 1 slice of bread, add cheese and sauerkraut. Spread mustard on second slice of bread and top sandwich. Place on panini press.

2. Close the lid and cook for 3–5 minutes. Remove from press and slice in half. Serve warm.

Tomato and Pesto Grilled Cheese Panini

The addition of pesto turns that regular grilled cheese into an Italian treat.

1. Preheat the panini press. Lay the mozzarella cheese on 1 slice of bread. Add the tomato and Pesto Sauce and cover with the other slice of bread.

2. Place on panini press, close lid, and cook for 3–5 minutes.

3. Remove from press, cut in half, and serve warm.

Grilled Cheese with Mango Chutney

You've probably tried mango chutney on fish while visiting an exotic island. Mango chutney is also a fun addition to a regular old grilled cheese. You'll feel like you're on vacation with every bite.

1. Preheat the panini press. Lay pepper jack cheese on 1 slice of bread. Add the mango chutney.

2. Place the other slice of bread on top and place on panini press.

3. Close lid and cook for 3–5 minutes.

4. Remove from press, cut in half, and serve warm.

Goat Cheese, Monterey Jack, and Bacon Panini

Try to find a premium bacon, which will add a smoky flavor to this grilled cheese panini.

1. Preheat the panini press. Cook bacon on the panini press until crisp.

2. Wearing an oven mitt, wipe bacon grease from panini press with a wad of paper towels.

3. Arrange goat cheese on 1 slice of bread and top with jack cheese. Add the bacon and Salsa.

4. Close the sandwich. Place on panini press, close lid, and cook for 3–5 minutes.

5. Remove from press, cut in half, and serve warm.

CHAPTER 6

Chicken and Turkey Panini

2 slices pumpernickel or rye bread

3 slices turkey

1 chopped scallion

3 tablespoons cranberry sauce

¼ cup watercress lettuce

2 teaspoons mustard

1 tablespoon mayonnaise

Turkey and Cranberry Sauce Panini

You don't have to wait for Thanksgiving to enjoy turkey and cranberry sauce. With the help of your panini press, you can make this sandwich any time of the year.

1. Preheat the panini press. On 1 slice of bread, add turkey, scallion, cranberry sauce, and watercress lettuce. Spread mustard and mayonnaise on the other slice of bread and top sandwich.

2. Place on panini press and close the lid.

3. Cook for 3–5 minutes. Remove from press and slice in half. Serve warm.

Variation

Why not include more of those Thanksgiving leftovers in this panini? Add a few spoonfuls of stuffing! Red onion slices are also a great addition.

1 or 2 thin-sliced chicken breasts

Salt and pepper, to taste

1 sandwich-sized baguette

3 slices ham

3 slices provolone

2 tablespoons mayonnaise

Chicken, Ham, and Provolone Panini

This is a perfect hot sandwich for a weekend lunch at home. And if you have leftover chicken breast in the fridge, you're only a few minutes away from lunch.

1. Preheat the panini press. Place chicken breast on panini press. Sprinkle with salt and pepper before closing lid. Cook for 4–6 minutes, depending on thickness of the chicken breast. Remove from panini press and set aside.

2. Cut a baguette lengthwise and open it up. Add chicken, ham, and provolone. Spread mayonnaise on the top half of the baguette and close sandwich.

3. Place on panini press and close the lid.

4. Cook for 3–5 minutes. Remove from press and slice in half. Serve warm.

1 or 2 thin-sliced chicken breasts

Salt and pepper, to taste

2 slices Italian bread

2 tablespoons sun-dried tomatoes

2 slices prosciutto

1 tablespoon grated Parmesan cheese

Chicken, Prosciutto, and Sun-Dried Tomato Panini

Sun-dried tomatoes are sold by the jar, packed in oil or dry. The sun-dried tomatoes packed in oil are perfect for panini sandwiches.

1. Preheat the panini press. Place chicken breast on panini press. Sprinkle with salt and pepper before closing lid. Cook for 4–6 minutes, depending on thickness of the chicken breast. Remove from panini press and set aside.

2. On 1 slice of bread, add chicken, sun-dried tomatoes, prosciutto, and Parmesan cheese. Top the sandwich with another slice of bread.

3. Place on panini press and close the lid.

4. Cook for 3–5 minutes. Remove from press and slice in half. Serve warm.

Reconstituting Sun-Dried Tomatoes

Sun-dried tomatoes that are packed in oil are panini-ready and can be added straight from the jar. Sun-dried tomatoes that are packed dry will taste like shoe leather, so follow these steps to get them panini-ready. Place sun-dried tomatoes in a heatproof bowl and pour boiling water over them until they are covered. Let sit for 10–15 minutes until soft.

1 or 2 chicken cutlets

2 slices honey oatmeal bread

¼ cup apple butter or jelly

1 tablespoon honey

½ teaspoon cinnamon

¼ teaspoon nutmeg

¼ teaspoon salt

Apple Cinnamon Chicken Panini

Wait until autumn and buy some fresh apple butter from a farm or farmer's market to use instead of regular apple jelly. It's worth the wait.

1. Preheat the panini press. Cook the chicken cutlets on panini press for 3–6 minutes.

2. Arrange chicken pieces on 1 slice of bread and add apple butter, honey, cinnamon, nutmeg, and salt. Close sandwich with the other slice of bread and place on panini press.

3. Close lid and cook for 3–5 minutes.

4. Remove from press, cut in half, and serve warm.

Variations

The addition of chopped pecans to this dish makes for a heartier panini. You can chop whole pecans with a knife on a cutting board or use the pulse feature of your food processor. Do not chop them too fine or you will create pecan dust.

Teriyaki Chicken Panini

Teriyaki chicken is tasty served many different ways. In this panini the red onions go nicely with the teriyaki flavor.

1. Preheat the panini press. Cook chicken cutlets on panini press for 4–6 minutes. Remove from press and set aside.

2. On 1 slice of bread add the chicken, onion, and teriyaki sauce. Top with the other slice of bread.

3. Place on panini press, close lid, and cook for 2–4 minutes.

4. Remove from press, cut in half, and serve warm.

Turkey Chili Panini

You've probably tried turkey chili before, but have you tried turkey with chili? Adding chili is a great way to add lots of extra flavor to a turkey panini and use up some leftovers at the same time.

1. Preheat the panini press. Cut open the hard rolls and scoop out some bread to form a pocket. Add the turkey and cheese. Scoop on some chili and add the onions. Close roll and place on panini press.

2. Close the lid and cook for 2–4 minutes. Remove from press and serve warm.

1 tablespoon chili powder

1 teaspoon thyme

1 tablespoon onion powder

1 tablespoon garlic powder

1 teaspoon white pepper

1 teaspoon salt

2 chicken cutlets

2 slices sourdough bread

2 slices tomato

3 slices Monterey jack cheese

1 tablespoon Chipotle Mayonnaise (see Chapter 19)

Tex-Mex Chicken Panini

Boneless chicken breasts are a great item to buy in bulk and stock up on. There are so many different ways to season and marinate them that you'll never get bored of having a chicken panini.

1. Preheat the panini press. In a bowl combine chili powder, thyme, onion powder, garlic powder, pepper, and salt and mix well. Rub the spices on the chicken cutlets and grill on panini press for 4–6 minutes.

2. Cut chicken into slices if desired and place on 1 slice of bread along with the tomato and cheese. Spread the Chipotle Mayonnaise on the other slice of bread and top the panini.

3. Place on panini press, close lid, and cook for 3–5 minutes.

4. Remove from press, cut in half, and serve warm.

2 tablespoons onion powder

2 teaspoons thyme

2 teaspoons allspice

2 teaspoons black pepper

1 teaspoon cinnamon

½ teaspoon cayenne pepper

½ teaspoon salt

2 chicken cutlets

2 slices whole-grain bread

1 tablespoon mango chutney

2–3 romaine lettuce leaves

Jamaican Jerk Chicken Panini

There's no need to wait for your next vacation to enjoy some jerk seasoning. Mango chutney can be found in most supermarkets in the international section.

1. Preheat the panini press. In a bowl combine onion powder, thyme, allspice, black pepper, cinnamon, cayenne pepper, and salt and mix well. Rub the spices on the chicken cutlets and grill on panini press for 4–6 minutes.

2. Cut chicken into slices if desired and place on 1 slice of bread along with the mango chutney and lettuce. Close the sandwich.

3. Place on panini press, close lid, and cook for 3–5 minutes.

4. Remove from press, cut in half, and serve warm.

Barbecue Turkey Panini

2 slices sourdough bread

2 tablespoons barbecue sauce

4 slices cooked turkey

3 slices Swiss cheese

2 tablespoons hot and sweet peppers

2 slices onion

Variation

You don't have to wait until the holidays to make this panini with leftover turkey. Rotisserie chicken can fill in for the turkey. You don't even have to cook it yourself. Many supermarkets sell fully-cooked rotisserie chicken in their carryout sections.

Leave the gravy for another time and load up this turkey with barbecue sauce. You may want to update your post-Thanksgiving leftovers after you taste this panini.

1. Preheat the panini press. On 1 slice of bread, spread the barbecue sauce and arrange the turkey and Swiss cheese. Add the peppers and onion. Close sandwich with the other slice of bread.

2. Place on panini press, close lid, and cook for 3–5 minutes.

3. Remove from press, cut in half, and serve warm.

Turkey Reuben Panini

2 slices rye bread

5 slices turkey

2 slices Swiss cheese

¼ cup sauerkraut

2 tablespoons Russian dressing

A reuben can be made a lot healthier by using fresh oven-roasted turkey instead of corned beef or pastrami.

1. On 1 slice of rye bread, add turkey, cheese, and sauerkraut. Spread Russian dressing the other slice and close sandwich.

2. Place on panini press, close lid, and cook for 3–5 minutes.

3. Remove from press, cut in half, and serve warm.

2 chicken cutlets
½ zucchini, sliced
½ eggplant, chopped
4–6 mushrooms, sliced
2 tablespoons olive oil
2 tablespoons minced garlic
Salt and pepper, to taste
2 slices crusty bread
3 slices mozzarella cheese

Chicken and Veggies Panini

If the stars of this panini are the vegetables, that would make the chicken the special guest star. Use a big crusty bread to hold it all together.

1. Preheat the panini press. Place chicken on panini press, close lid, and cook for 4–6 minutes. Remove from press and set aside.

2. Place zucchini, eggplant, and mushrooms in a bowl. Drizzle with olive oil. Add garlic, salt, and pepper. Mix well and pour contents of bowl onto panini press. Cook for 3–6 minutes.

3. On 1 slice of bread add the grilled vegetables. Slice the chicken into bite-sized pieces and add to the panini. Add the cheese and top with another slice of bread.

4. Place on panini press, close lid, and cook for 3–5 minutes.

5. Remove from press, cut in half, and serve warm.

Hold in the Juices

When cooking meat such as chicken breast or steaks on a panini press, you should always let the meat sit for a few minutes before cutting it. If you cut it immediately after cooking, all of the juices will run out, and those juices are responsible for a lot of flavor. By letting the meat sit for a while, you'll trap in more liquid and more flavor.

1 boneless chicken breast

Salt and pepper, to taste

2 tablespoons teriyaki sauce

3 slices pineapple

1 hamburger roll

Grilled Chicken and Pineapple Panini

A healthier option to ground beef hamburgers is a grilled chicken breast. And what goes better with chicken than teriyaki sauce and grilled pineapple?

1. Preheat the panini press. Place chicken breast on panini press. Sprinkle with salt and pepper before closing lid. Cook for 4–6 minutes, depending on thickness of the chicken breast. Remove from panini press and set aside.

2. In a bowl add teriyaki sauce and pineapple slices. Mix until evenly coated. Shake excess sauce off of pineapple slices and grill on panini press for 1–2 minutes.

3. Spread remaining teriyaki sauce on both sides of roll and add cooked chicken breast and pineapple slices. Close roll.

4. Place on panini press, close lid, and cook for additional 2–3 minutes.

5. Remove from panini press and serve warm.

Cooking Chicken Safely

Raw chicken can contain salmonella. When cooking chicken breast in your panini press, be sure to cook it away from any other ingredients to avoid contamination. Be sure to clean the panini press really well before using it again.

Barbecue Chicken Panini

The onion rings will look a little funny if your panini press has ridges on the cooking surface, but don't worry because they'll be hidden inside the sandwich.

1. Preheat the panini press. Place chicken breast on panini press. Sprinkle with salt and pepper before closing lid. Cook for 4–6 minutes, depending on thickness of the chicken breast. Remove from panini press and set aside.

2. Place onion rings and bacon on the panini press and close lid. Cook for 3–5 minutes depending on size of onion rings and bacon. Remove both from panini press and set aside.

3. Put chicken inside the roll and lay the bacon, onion rings, and cheese on top. Next spread the barbecue sauce on the top of the roll and close the sandwich. Place it back on panini press, close lid, and cook for an additional 1–2 minutes.

4. Remove from press and serve hot.

Variation

A buttery brioche roll can be used instead of a hamburger roll. Or to really turn this panini into something different, use a roasted red pepper focaccia and save the rolls for hamburgers.

1 or 2 chicken cutlets

Salt and pepper, to taste

1 cup broccoli raab, chopped

2 tablespoons olive oil

2 tablespoons minced garlic

1 long roll

2 tablespoons Olive Tapenade (see Chapter 19)

Grilled Chicken and Broccoli Raab Panini

Broccoli raab isn't just for sausage sandwiches and pasta dishes. You can use it in many different panini.

1. Preheat panini press. Place chicken cutlets on panini press. Sprinkle with salt and pepper before closing lid. Cook for 4–6 minutes, depending on thickness of the chicken breast. Remove from panini press and set aside.

2. In a pot of boiling water, blanch the broccoli raab for 2–3 minutes. Remove from water and submerge in an ice bath. Drain the raab in a colander. In a bowl combine broccoli raab, olive oil, and garlic. Pour contents of bowl on panini press and cook for 3–5 minutes.

3. Cut open a long roll lengthwise and add the chicken and the broccoli raab. Spoon on the Olive Tapenade and close roll.

4. Place on panini press, close lid, and cook for 3–5 minutes.

5. Remove from press, cut in half, and serve warm.

Variations

Mozzarella cheese is a good addition to this panini.

INGREDIENTS | SERVES 1

3 slices bacon

1–2 thin chicken cutlets

2 slices whole wheat bread

2 slices tomato

2 slices onion

3 tablespoons Guacamole (see Chapter 19)

Grilled Chicken, Bacon, and Guacamole Panini

Fresh guacamole is a great addition to any panini, but if you don't have any, a few slices of ripe avocado will do in a pinch.

1. Preheat the panini press. Cook bacon in panini press until crisp and set aside.

2. Place chicken cutlets on panini grill, close lid, and cook for 3–5 minutes.

3. Cut chicken into strips and arrange on 1 slice of bread. Add the bacon, tomato, and onion. Spoon a generous portion of Guacamole on top of the other ingredients and close sandwich.

4. Place on the panini press, close lid, and cook for 2–4 minutes.

5. Cut in half and serve warm.

CHAPTER 7

Fish and Seafood Panini

Shrimp, Feta, and Black Olive Panini

Feta cheese comes in both block form and crumbled. The crumbled variety is much easier to use for panini making.

1. Preheat the panini press. Place the shrimp on panini press, close lid, and cook for 2–3 minutes. Remove from press and set aside.

2. On 1 slice of bread add the shrimp, feta cheese, black olives, and red onion. Add salt and pepper to taste. Drizzle the olive oil and red wine vinegar on another slice of bread and top sandwich.

3. Place on panini press and close the lid.

4. Cook for 3–5 minutes. Remove from press and slice in half. Serve warm.

Fresh Shrimp

When buying shrimp at the fish market the smell is very important. Your shrimp shouldn't smell like anything other than salt water. If there is a slight scent of ammonia, that means that the shrimp is past its prime.

2 tablespoons Dijon mustard

1 swordfish steak

2 slices whole wheat bread

3 slices tomato

2 slices red onion

2 slices red pepper

Dijon Swordfish Panini

If it's too cold outside to fire up the barbecue for some grilled fish, you can always fire up the panini press.

1. Preheat the panini press. Spread mustard on one side of swordfish steak, and place it mustard side down on panini press. Spread additional mustard on the top of the swordfish and then close the lid. Cook for 2–4 minutes, depending on the thickness of the fish. Remove from press and place on 1 slice of bread. Cut fish into bite-sized chunks if desired. Add tomato, red onion, and red pepper and close sandwich.

2. Place on panini press, close lid, and cook for 2–3 minutes.

3. Remove from press, cut in half, and serve warm.

Swordfish

Swordfish got their name because their snout is similar to the shape of a sword. The average swordfish weighs between 190 and 330 pounds, but the largest recorded swordfish weight is well over 1,000 pounds!

1 tilapia fillet

2 tablespoons olive oil

2 slices bread

3 slices tomato

2 slices red onion

2 tablespoons Cilantro Lime Mayonnaise (see Chapter 19)

Cilantro Lime Tilapia Panini

Try to get an Italian panella loaf for this panini and cut it thick. There's enough flavor to use a lot of bread.

1. Preheat the panini press. Place the tilapia fillet on panini press and drizzle with olive oil. Close lid and cook for 2–4 minutes. Remove from press and place on 1 slice of bread. Cut fish into bite-sized chunks if desired. Add tomato and red onion. Spread Cilantro Lime Mayonnaise on the other slice of bread and close sandwich.

2. Place on panini press, close lid, and cook for 2–3 minutes.

3. Remove from press, cut in half, and serve warm.

Cilantro and Coriander

Cilantro and coriander may taste very differently, but they come from the same plant. The leaves of the plant are used for cilantro and the seeds are used for coriander.

10 medium shrimp, peeled and deveined

2 tablespoons olive oil

2 tablespoons minced garlic

1 long roll

1 tablespoon Parmesan cheese

1 cup shredded arugula

Variation

Sometimes arugula is hard to find at your local supermarket. If you have trouble finding it you can replace it with endive, escarole, or dandelion greens.

Garlic Shrimp and Arugula Panini

Arugula is also known as rocket, roquette, rucchetta, and rucola. It's very popular in Italian cuisine.

1. Preheat the panini press. In a bowl combine the shrimp, olive oil, and garlic and mix well. Pour contents of bowl onto panini press, close lid, and cook for 2–3 minutes.

2. Cut open a long roll and add shrimp, Parmesan cheese, and arugula. Place on panini press, close lid, and cook for 2–4 minutes.

3. Remove from press, cut in half, and serve warm.

INGREDIENTS | SERVES 1

1 frozen breaded white fish fillet

2 slices sourdough bread

2 slices onion

2 slices tomato

½ teaspoon horseradish

2 tablespoons tartar sauce

Fish Fillet Panini

You can skip the drive-through window the next time you have a craving for a fish fillet sandwich. And the addition of fresh vegetables makes this fish fillet a meal.

1. Cook fish fillet in oven according to instructions on package.

2. Preheat the panini press. On 1 slice of bread, add fish fillet, onion, tomato, horseradish, and tartar sauce. Close the sandwich.

3. Place on panini press, close lid, and cook for 3–5 minutes.

4. Remove from press, cut in half, and serve warm.

4 jalapeño peppers
¼ cup lump crabmeat
2 slices onion
3 slices roasted red peppers
2 slices bread
1 tablespoon Dijon mustard

Jalapeño Crab Panini

A big crunchy ciabatta roll or thick slices of Italian bread are perfect for this spicy crabby patty.

1. Preheat the panini press. Place the jalapeño peppers on panini press and close lid. Cook for 3–5 minutes. Remove from press and place on a cutting board. Scrape off any black char marks and cut into slices. Remove seeds and stems.

2. Lay jalapeño slices, crabmeat, onion, and roasted peppers on 1 slice of bread. Spread the mustard on the other slice of bread and close sandwich.

3. Place on panini press, close lid, and cook for 3–4 minutes.

4. Remove from press and cut in half. Serve warm.

Variation

Cooked and chopped shrimp can be used instead of lump crabmeat in this panini. The taste will definitely be different, but it will still be good.

1 (4-ounce) salmon fillet
½ zucchini, sliced
½ eggplant, chopped
4–6 mushrooms, sliced
2 tablespoons olive oil
2 tablespoons minced garlic
Salt and pepper, to taste
2 slices whole-grain bread
3 slices mozzarella cheese

Salmon and Veggie Panini

Adding grilled vegetables to a fish-based panini is a great recipe for a delicious meal. Don't be afraid to experiment with whatever vegetables you have in your fridge. Most of them are waiting for you to break out the panini press.

1. Preheat the panini press. Place salmon fillet on panini press, close lid, and grill for 4–6 minutes; set aside.

2. Place zucchini, eggplant, and mushrooms in a bowl. Drizzle with olive oil, and add garlic, salt, and pepper. Mix well, and pour contents of bowl onto panini press. Close lid and cook for 3–6 minutes.

3. On 1 slice of bread add the grilled vegetables. Break up salmon fillet with a fork and add the pieces to the panini. Add the cheese, and top with another slice of bread.

4. Place on panini press, close lid, and cook for 3–5 minutes.

5. Remove from press, cut in half, and serve warm.

Variation

Some other vegetables that you might enjoy grilled on your panini press would be summer squash, asparagus, bell peppers, or onions. Go to a farmers' market and don't be afraid to do some experimenting.

4 tablespoons soy sauce

1 (4-ounce) tuna steak

1 tablespoon sesame seeds

2 teaspoons wasabi mayonnaise

2 slices Italian bread or a ciabatta roll

Grilled Tuna with Wasabi Panini

Don't overcook your tuna or it will dry out. It should still be pink in the middle when it's done.

1. Preheat the panini press. Pour the soy sauce in a bowl and place the tuna steak in it. Flip the steak over to get a good soaking in the soy sauce. Place tuna steak on panini press and sprinkle sesame seeds on top. Close lid and sear for 1–2 minutes. Tuna steak should still be red inside when finished. Remove from press and set aside.

2. Spread wasabi mayonnaise on 1 slice of bread.

3. Break up tuna steak with a fork and add pieces on sandwich. Close the sandwich.

4. Place on panini press, close lid, and cook for 1–2 minutes.

5. Remove from press, cut in half, and serve warm with a bowl of soy sauce for dipping.

Variations

Asian salad greens such as mizuna and red mustard are a good addition to this panini. Also try it with green onions.

CHAPTER 8

Salad Panini

1 or 2 chicken cutlets
2 tablespoons Caesar dressing
2 slices whole wheat bread
1 tablespoon Parmesan cheese
2–3 leaves romaine lettuce
2 slices tomato

Chicken Caesar Panini

Many popular salads make for nice panini sandwiches. Use thickly sliced bread if you want to load up on the dressing.

1. Preheat the panini press. Place chicken cutlets on panini press, close lid, and cook for 4–6 minutes. Remove from press and set aside.

2. Add the Caesar salad dressing to 1 slice of bread. Add the Parmesan cheese, romaine lettuce, and tomato slices. Cut the chicken into slices and add to panini, then close the sandwich.

3. Place on panini press, close lid, and cook for 2–4 minutes.

4. Remove from press, cut in half, and serve warm.

2 cups cubed chicken breast (cooked)
1 stalk celery, finely chopped
½ cup chopped onion
½ cup mayonnaise
1 teaspoon parsley, chopped
1 teaspoon Dijon mustard
Salt and pepper, to taste
¼ teaspoon celery seed
1 teaspoon lemon juice
4 slices whole wheat bread

Chicken Salad Panini

Add more celery and onion if you want a crunchier chicken salad, and more mayonnaise if you like it creamier.

1. Preheat the panini press. Mix all ingredients except the bread in a bowl.

2. Spread the mixture between 2 slices of bread, top with the remaining 2 slices of bread, and place on panini press. Close lid and cook for 2–3 minutes.

3. Remove from press and slice in half. Serve warm.

Variations

Try adding sliced tomato and lettuce greens to the panini before putting it in the press. Bacon will also go nicely with this panini.

INGREDIENTS | **SERVES 1**

3 strips bacon

1 hard-boiled egg, sliced

2 slices Italian bread or a ciabatta roll

¼ cup grated Roquefort cheese

1 small bunch romaine lettuce

1 small bunch watercress lettuce

1 sliced avocado

1 sliced tomato

1 tablespoon chopped chives

1 tablespoon red wine vinaigrette dressing

Cobb Salad Panini

If you don't have Roquefort cheese on hand, you can substitute crumbled blue cheese or Gorgonzola. The thickness of your bread will determine how much of the salad greens you can pile on.

1. Preheat the panini press. Cook bacon on panini press until crisp and set aside.

2. Arrange hard-boiled egg slices on 1 slice of bread. Sprinkle the Roquefort cheese on top. Add the romaine and watercress lettuces, avocado slices, tomato slices, bacon, and chives.

3. Drizzle the red wine vinaigrette dressing on the second slice of bread. Top sandwich and place on panini press. Close lid and cook for 3–4 minutes.

4. Remove from press and slice in half. Serve warm.

Cobb Salad History

Some say that the Cobb salad was invented at a restaurant called the Hollywood Brown Derby, in Hollywood, California, in the 1930s. However, some people dispute this and claim the salad came from Nebraska almost two decades earlier.

3 strips bacon

1 hard-boiled egg, sliced

2 slices Italian bread or a ciabatta roll

¼ cup grated Roquefort cheese

1 cooked boneless chicken breast

1 small bunch romaine lettuce

1 small bunch watercress lettuce

1 sliced avocado

1 sliced tomato

1 tablespoon chopped chives

1 tablespoon red wine vinaigrette dressing

1 teaspoon Worcestershire sauce

Chicken Cobb Panini

The traditional Cobb salad is usually made with chicken. For a spicier panini, add a dash of hot sauce or Worcestershire sauce.

1. Preheat the panini press. Cook bacon on panini press until crisp and set aside.

2. Arrange hard-boiled egg slices on 1 slice of bread. Sprinkle the Roquefort cheese on top and then add the chicken breast, romaine and watercress lettuces, avocado slices, tomato slices, bacon, and chives.

3. Drizzle the red wine vinaigrette dressing and the Worcestershire sauce on the second slice of bread. Top sandwich and place on panini press. Close lid and cook for 3–4 minutes.

4. Remove from press and slice in half. Serve warm.

Variations

Blue cheese or Gorgonzola can be used instead of the Roquefort cheese.

1 teaspoon vinegar

4 eggs

1 tablespoon mayonnaise

2 tablespoons Dijon mustard

½ red onion

1 teaspoon paprika

Salt and pepper, to taste

4 slices whole wheat bread

Egg Salad Panini

Use less mayonnaise than you normally would when making regular egg salad. The heat from the panini press will keep the sandwich moist. You could try it with rye bread, too.

1. In a pot of boiling water add vinegar and hard boil eggs. Cook for 10 minutes, and then remove from heat and let the eggs sit in the pot for another 10 minutes. Remove from water and let them cool before peeling and chopping.

2. Preheat the panini press. In a bowl combine the chopped eggs, mayonnaise, Dijon mustard, red onion, paprika, salt, and pepper. Mash well with a fork.

3. Spread the egg mixture between 2 slices of bread and place on panini press. Close lid and cook for 2–3 minutes.

4. Remove from press and slice in half. Serve warm.

Peeling Hard-Boiled Eggs

Peeling a hard-boiled egg is a messy and time-consuming job. If you add a teaspoon of baking soda to the water before boiling the eggs, it will raise the pH of the water and loosen the egg shell. This will make it easier to peel.

2 cups shredded chicken breast (cooked)
⅓ cup mayonnaise
⅓ cup sour cream
1 teaspoon orange juice
½ teaspoon grated ginger
1 teaspoon curry powder
½ cup chopped celery
¼ cup chopped green onion
1 peeled and chopped apple
Salt and pepper, to taste
4 slices whole grain bread

Curry Chicken Salad Panini

If regular chicken salad seems a little boring to you, then this variation with curry should be right up your alley.

1. Preheat the panini press. Mix all ingredients except the bread in a bowl.

2. Divide the mixture between 2 slices of bread, and close sandwiches. Place on panini press. Close lid and cook for 2–3 minutes.

3. Remove from press and slice in half. Serve warm.

What Is Curry?

Turmeric, coriander, and cumin are the spices most commonly found in curry powder, but it can vary based on your location. Sometimes ginger, garlic, or fennel can be added as well. Curry powder is mostly used in South Asian cuisine.

Tuna Melt Panini

To keep the tuna salad and tomato from sliding out from under the bread, surround them with Swiss cheese on both the top and bottom of this panini.

1. Preheat the panini press. Place the tuna, mayonnaise, onion, celery, lemon juice, hot sauce, and parsley in a bowl and mash with a fork until well mixed.

2. Place the Swiss cheese on both pieces of bread. Spread the mixture on top of the cheese on 1 slice of bread, and top with tomato. Close the sandwich, and place on panini press. Close lid and cook for 2–3 minutes.

3. Remove from press and slice in half. Serve warm.

Variations

To give this panini a more gourmet punch, replace the canned tuna with a grilled tuna steak. Use the panini press to sear the tuna steak for 1–2 minutes, and break it apart with a fork.

6 ounces lump crabmeat

¼ cup mayonnaise

1 teaspoon lemon juice

2 tablespoons chopped red onion

4 slices white or wheat bread

1 sliced cucumber

Cucumber Crab Panini

Seedless cucumbers should be used to give this panini more of a crunch.

1. Preheat the panini press. In a bowl combine lump crab, mayonnaise, lemon juice, and red onion and mix with a fork.

2. Divide the crab mixture between 2 slices of bread and then add the cucumber slices. Top the sandwiches with the other slices of bread and place on panini press.

3. Close the lid and cook for 2–3 minutes.

4. Remove from press and slice in half. Serve warm.

Imitation Crabmeat

Imitation crab is usually made using Alaskan pollock. The fish is processed and artificially flavored to give it an appealing texture and crablike flavor. Caramel and paprika are commonly used to give imitation crab its red or pink coloring.

INGREDIENTS | SERVES 1

1 pear, cut into ¼" slices

2 slices honey oat bread

2 tablespoons crumbled feta

¼ cup spinach leaves

2 teaspoons chopped and roasted walnuts

2 tablespoons cream cheese

1 tablespoon balsamic vinegar

Pear, Spinach, and Walnut Panini

A food processor can be used to easily chop walnuts.

1. Preheat the panini press. Lay pear slices on top of 1 slice of bread. Add feta cheese, spinach, and roasted walnuts.

2. Spread the cream cheese on the other slice of bread and then drizzle with balsamic vinegar. Top sandwich and place on panini press.

3. Close the lid and cook for 3–5 minutes. Remove from press and slice in half. Serve warm.

Roasting Nuts

Nuts taste better when they're roasted. Whether it's walnuts, pine nuts, or even peanuts, they will enhance your panini's flavor. To roast small nuts, place them in a frying pan. Heat for a few minutes over a medium flame while mixing the nuts so that they don't burn. Larger nuts should be chopped before using this method.

Pear, Goat Cheese, and Prosciutto Panini

INGREDIENTS | SERVES 1

1 pear, cut into ¼" slices
2 slices Italian bread
3 tablespoons goat cheese
3 slices prosciutto
3 slices red onion
1 teaspoon balsamic vinegar

Variations

Bresaola is an Italian specialty that is made by air-curing beef. If you don't eat pork, then substitute the prosciutto with bresaola.

Feel free to add more prosciutto to this panini if it's sliced really thin. If using Italian bread for this recipe, cut it thin.

1. Preheat the panini press. Lay pear slices on top of 1 slice of bread. Add goat cheese, prosciutto, and red onion.

2. Drizzle another slice of bread with balsamic vinegar and top sandwich. Place on panini press.

3. Close the lid and cook for 3–5 minutes. Remove from press and slice in half. Serve warm.

Horiatiki Panini

INGREDIENTS | SERVES 1

2 slices Kalamata olive bread
2 tablespoons olive oil
3 slices tomato
2 slices green pepper
¼ cup feta cheese
6 cucumber slices
¼ cup chopped Kalamata olives
3 slices red onion
Salt and pepper, to taste

This popular Greek salad gets a panini makeover. Just add crusty bread.

1. Preheat the panini press. Lay 2 slices of bread on the counter and drizzle with olive oil.

2. Add the rest of the ingredients to 1 slice of bread and close sandwich with the other slice.

3. Place on panini press, close lid, and cook for 3–5 minutes.

4. Remove from press, slice in half, and serve warm.

1–2 slices cantaloupe or honeydew melon, rind removed

2 slices Italian bread

3 slices prosciutto

3 slices mozzarella cheese

2 tablespoons olive oil

Growing Melon

You'll need plenty of room to grow melon in your home garden. The vines can take over a small space pretty quickly. Try using a trellis to grow melons vertically.

Melon, Prosciutto, and Mozzarella Panini

Melon and prosciutto are often served with mini mozzarella balls in a salad or as appetizers. Why not move it to the main course?

1. Preheat the panini press. Lay the melon slices on 1 slice of bread. Add the prosciutto and mozzarella cheese.

2. Drizzle oil on another slice of bread and top sandwich.

3. Place on panini press and close the lid.

4. Cook for 3–5 minutes. Remove from press and slice in half. Serve warm.

1–2 slices cantaloupe melon, rind removed

2 slices Italian bread

3 slices prosciutto

3 slices fontina cheese

1 teaspoon balsamic vinegar

4–6 basil leaves

1 tablespoon olive oil

Prosciutto, Melon, and Fontina Panini

Fontina is a delicious white cheese that's perfect for melting. It will become the creamy filling of your favorite sandwiches.

1. Lay the melon slices on 1 slice of bread. Add the prosciutto and fontina cheese. Drizzle with balsamic vinegar and add basil leaves.

2. Drizzle oil on another slice of bread and top sandwich.

3. Place on panini press and close the lid.

4. Cook for 3–5 minutes. Remove from press and slice in half. Serve warm.

CHAPTER 9

Vegetarian Panini

1 small eggplant, sliced about ¼" thick

¼–½ cup crumbled feta cheese

2 slices Italian bread or ciabatta roll

1 teaspoon balsamic vinegar

Salt and pepper, to taste.

Eggplant and Feta Panini

When it comes to vegetable sandwiches, eggplant is the MVP. If you learn how to properly cook eggplant on a panini press, you'll be very happy with any eggplant panini. Try this panini on a ciabatta roll or thick crusty bread.

1. Preheat the panini press. Place eggplant on panini press, close lid, and cook for 3–5 minutes. Remove eggplant from press and set aside.

2. Place eggplant and feta cheese on a slice of bread or the bottom half of a roll. Drizzle balsamic vinegar on the top half of roll and let it soak in. Sprinkle with salt and pepper, and then put the two halves together.

3. Place on panini press and close lid.

4. Cook for 3–5 minutes and remove from press.

5. Cut in half and serve warm.

Degorging Eggplants

Have you ever had a bitter-tasting eggplant? Sometimes eggplant, especially the large seedy ones, need to be salted and pressed to improve their flavor. This process is called degorging or purging, and it's easy to do. Slice your eggplant and lay the pieces on a few layers of paper towels. Sprinkle with salt and add a cover of more paper towels. Next, you should place a baking sheet on top of the eggplant. The salt will cause the eggplant to "sweat" a brown bitter liquid. This is what you want to get rid of. The paper towels will also absorb any excess moisture to avoid a mushy cooked eggplant. Let the salted eggplant sit for about 30 minutes, then rinse and pat dry with more paper towels.

Eggplant, Pepper, and Pesto Panini

You can't go wrong with pesto and goat cheese.

1. Preheat the panini press. Place eggplant on panini press, close lid, and cook for 3–5 minutes. Remove the eggplant from the press and lay it on top of 1 slice of bread.

2. Add the goat cheese and the roasted pepper. Spread the Pesto Sauce onto a second slice of bread, and place on top of sandwich pesto side down.

3. Place on panini press, close lid, and cook for about 3–5 minutes.

4. Remove from press, slice in half, and serve warm.

Zucchini, Pepper, and Olive Panini

Looking for a lighter panini? Put all the ingredients on a flour tortilla to make a panini wrap.

1. Preheat the panini press. Place sliced zucchini on panini press and drizzle with olive oil. Close the lid and cook for 3–5 minutes. Remove zucchini from press and place on 1 slice of bread.

2. Add the pepper slices and the green olives and top sandwich with another slice of bread.

3. Place on panini press, close lid, and cook for 3–5 minutes.

4. Remove from press, slice in half, and serve warm.

1 small onion, chopped or sliced

2 teaspoons olive oil

Salt and pepper, to taste

2 slices Italian bread

3 slices Brie cheese

Caramelized Onion and Brie Panini

Caramelizing an onion almost makes it taste like a different vegetable altogether.

1. Preheat the panini press. Place onion on panini press. Drizzle with olive oil and add salt and pepper and then close the lid. Grill for 2–4 minutes and set aside.

2. On 1 slice of bread, place Brie cheese and top with caramelized onion.

3. Close sandwich and place on panini press. Close lid and cook for 3–5 minutes.

4. Remove from press, slice in half, and serve warm.

Variation

A suitable replacement for Brie cheese is Camembert cheese. They are both types of soft white cheese that originated in the south of France. Camembert has a slightly stronger flavor so you may want to use a little less of it.

2 slices Italian bread

1 zucchini, sliced about ¼" thick

3 slices mozzarella

3 slices tomato

1 tablespoon Pesto Sauce (see Chapter 19)

Zucchini, Mozzarella, and Tomato Panini

This panini is great with garden-fresh zucchini. You won't give away as many zucchini to neighbors after you've tried it.

1. Preheat the panini press. Place sliced zucchini on panini press, close lid, and cook for 3–5 minutes. Remove zucchini from press and set aside.

2. Add zucchini, mozzarella, and tomato to 1 slice of bread.

3. Spread Pesto Sauce onto second slice of bread, and place on top of sandwich with pesto side down.

4. Place on panini press, close lid, and cook for 3–5 minutes.

5. Remove from press, slice in half, and serve warm.

Variation

Try this recipe using yellow pattypan squash. Its mellow flavor makes a great substitute for zucchini, and it's so fun to look at. Leave a few uncooked to show off to your friends.

Portobello Mushroom and Arugula Panini

Chewy ciabatta bread will help you soak up all of the garlic and oil. You won't want to waste it.

1. Preheat the panini press. Place mushroom cap on panini press and drizzle with olive oil. Add minced garlic on top and close the lid. Cook for 3–5 minutes. Remove mushroom from press and set aside.

2. Add mushroom and arugula to 1 slice of bread, and cover with the other slice of bread.

3. Place on panini press, close lid, and cook for 3–5 minutes.

4. Remove from press, slice in half, and serve warm.

Avocado, Tomato, and Pepper Panini

Garden-fresh tomatoes and ripe avocados make all the difference in the world.

1. Preheat the panini press. Spread cream cheese on 1 slice of bread. Add sliced avocado, pepper, and tomato on top of the cream cheese.

2. Drizzle another slice of bread with balsamic vinegar and top the sandwich.

3. Place on panini press, close lid, and cook for 3–5 minutes.

4. Remove from press, slice in half, and serve warm.

INGREDIENTS | SERVES 1

2 teaspoons olive oil

1 small eggplant, sliced about ¼" thick

1 zucchini, sliced about ¼" thick

2 slices whole-grain bread

3 slices red onion

1 teaspoon balsamic vinegar

Salt and pepper, to taste

1 tablespoon mayonnaise

Eggplant, Zucchini, and Red Onion Panini

Try this recipe with a Japanese eggplant. They're less bitter and have fewer seeds.

1. Preheat the panini press. Brush or drizzle olive oil on eggplant and zucchini and place on panini press, close lid, and cook for 3–5 minutes. Remove zucchini and eggplant from press and lay onto 1 slice of bread.

2. Add red onion slices and drizzle balsamic vinegar, then add salt and pepper on top to taste.

3. Spread mayonnaise onto second slice of bread and place on top of sandwich with mayonnaise side down.

4. Place on panini press, close lid, and cook for 3–5 minutes.

5. Remove from press, slice in half, and serve warm.

Variation

Vegetable panini are a great opportunity to use focaccia as your bread. If you get a thick focaccia, slice it in half like a bagel and put your panini ingredients in between the two slices.

Broccoli Raab and Provolone Panini

Broccoli raab is an acquired taste, but once you acquire it, it'll be hard to get enough.

1. Preheat the panini press. In a bowl combine the olive oil, garlic, and broccoli raab. Mix to coat evenly with the oil. Pour contents on panini press, close lid, and cook for 3–5 minutes. Remove from press and arrange on 1 slice of bread.

2. Add provolone cheese and top with another slice of bread.

3. Place on panini press, close lid, and cook for 3–5 minutes.

4. Remove from press, slice in half, and serve warm.

Zucchini and Pesto Panini

Combining the flavor of basil and zucchini is something you'll want to do often.

1. Preheat the panini press. Place zucchini on panini press and drizzle with olive oil. Close the lid and cook for 3–5 minutes. Remove zucchini from press and place on 1 slice of bread.

2. Add the mozzarella cheese, spoon the Pesto Sauce on top of the sandwich, and close it with another slice of bread.

3. Place on panini press, close lid, and cook for 3–5 minutes.

4. Remove from press, slice in half, and serve warm.

Hummus and Pepper Panini

This recipe keeps it simple and tasty.

INGREDIENTS | SERVES 1

3 tablespoons hummus
2 slices whole-grain bread
½ green bell pepper
¼ cup arugula leaves

1. Preheat the panini press. Spread hummus on 1 slice of bread. Add green pepper and arugula leaves.

2. Top with the other slice of bread.

3. Place on panini press, close lid, and cook for 3–5 minutes.

4. Remove from press, slice in half, and serve warm.

Potato and Spinach Panini

If you're a fan of homemade pierogies but don't have the time to make them from scratch, this panini may satisfy your cravings. Leave the stand mixer in the closet for another day.

INGREDIENTS | SERVES 1

1 Kaiser roll
1 cup mashed potatoes
⅓ cup cooked spinach, drained
1 tablespoon sour cream
2 tablespoons shredded Cheddar cheese

1. Preheat panini press. Cut open the roll and layer the mashed potatoes, spinach, sour cream, and Cheddar cheese.

2. Place on preheated panini press and close the lid.

3. Cook for 3–5 minutes. Remove from press and slice in half. Serve warm.

INGREDIENTS | SERVES 1

4 slices eggplant, sliced about ¼" thick

1 tablespoon olive oil

2 slices Italian bread

4 slices roasted red pepper

1 tablespoon Garlic Mayonnaise (see Chapter 19)

Eggplant and Roasted Pepper Panini

Grilled eggplant and roasted peppers are good enough to eat by themselves. Add bread and garlic mayonnaise and put it all in the panini press and you've got something even better.

1. Preheat the panini press. Place eggplant on panini press and drizzle with olive oil. Close the lid and cook for 3–5 minutes. Remove eggplant from press and place on 1 slice of bread with the roasted pepper slices.

2. Spread the Garlic Mayonnaise on the other slice of bread. Close the sandwich.

3. Place on panini press, close lid, and cook for 3–5 minutes.

4. Remove from press, slice in half, and serve warm.

Focaccia

Here is another recipe that you'll want to try on focaccia. See if your bakery has any olive, roasted red pepper, or other varieties of focaccia that will complement this eggplant panini.

Panini with Cheese

Don't be afraid to load up on the cheeses in any of these recipes. They'll make your panini more gooey and delicious.

Sun-Dried Tomato, Ricotta, and Pesto Panini

Try this panini with a few different varieties of pesto, such as basil, spinach, or even arugula, to find your favorite. It'll be fun to try them all.

1. Preheat the panini press. Spread ricotta cheese on 1 slice of bread. Add sun-dried tomato slices on top.

2. Spoon the Pesto Sauce onto the other bread slice, and close the sandwich.

3. Place on panini press, close lid, and cook for 3–5 minutes.

4. Remove from press, slice in half, and serve warm.

Portobello with Blue Cheese Panini

Crumbled blue cheese or feta cheese gives this panini a creamy center. Be sure to load up with it.

1. Preheat the panini press. Place portobello mushroom cap on panini press. Drizzle with olive oil and sprinkle with garlic powder. Close lid and cook for 2–4 minutes.

2. Remove mushroom from press and place on a slice of bread. Add the blue cheese and baby spinach on top, and close the sandwich.

3. Place on panini press, close lid, and cook for 2–4 minutes.

4. Remove from press and cut in half. Serve warm.

1 sweet potato

3 tablespoons cream cheese

¼ teaspoon cinnamon

1 teaspoon maple syrup

2 slices honey oat bread or egg bread

Sweet Potato Panini

Sweet potatoes and yams are not related botanically, but either will do just fine in this recipe.

1. Wash the sweet potato, and pierce with a fork or knife. Bake sweet potato in the oven at 350°F for 1 hour. Remove from oven and let it cool enough to be handled. Cut the sweet potato in half and scoop out inside. Discard the skin.

2. Preheat the panini press. In a bowl combine the sweet potato, cream cheese, cinnamon, and maple syrup. Stir with a fork until ingredients are well mixed.

3. Spread mixture on 1 slice of bread, and close the sandwich.

4. Place it on the panini press. Close the lid and cook for 2–3 minutes.

5. Remove from press and slice in half. Serve warm.

Maple Syrup

Did you know it takes thirty to forty gallons of maple sap to make one gallon of maple syrup? The tree sap is boiled down for hours, and its concentrated form is what you buy at the store as maple syrup.

INGREDIENTS | SERVES 2

¼ cup lime juice

2 tablespoons chopped garlic

1 tablespoon cilantro

2 tablespoons olive oil

1 teaspoon cumin

3 portobello mushroom caps

1 onion, sliced

1 bell pepper, sliced

4 flour tortillas

2 tablespoons Salsa (see Chapter 19)

3 tablespoons canned black beans, drained

2 tablespoons Guacamole (see Chapter 19)

Vegetable Fajita Panini

Fajitas don't always have to be about the meat. Vegetables taste just as good when marinated and grilled in a panini press.

1. In a container large enough to hold the mushrooms, combine the lime juice, garlic, cilantro, olive oil, and cumin and mix well. Add the mushroom caps and marinate for 15 minutes.

2. Preheat the panini press. Place the mushrooms on panini press, close lid, and cook for 3–5 minutes. Remove from press and let cool for a few minutes, then cut into slices.

3. Place onion and pepper on panini press. Close lid and grill for 2–4 minutes and set aside.

4. On each flour tortilla, add mushrooms, grilled onions and peppers, Salsa, black beans, and Guacamole. Fold tortilla into a half-moon shape and place on panini press.

5. Close lid and cook for 3–5 minutes. Remove from press and cut with pizza cutter. Serve warm with extra Salsa and sour cream.

1 eggplant, chopped

2 zucchini, chopped

1 onion, chopped

2 yellow peppers, chopped

2 tablespoons minced garlic

1 bay leaf, crumbled

2 tablespoons olive oil

Salt and pepper, to taste

4 ciabatta rolls

2 tablespoons tomato sauce

Ratatouille Panini

Leave out the tomato sauce when cooking the vegetables and you'll be able to avoid a major cleaning job. Spread it on the bread to keep things neat.

1. Preheat the panini press. Place the eggplant, zucchini, onion, and peppers in a bowl. Add the garlic and bay leaf and drizzle with olive oil. Sprinkle with salt and pepper and mix well until the ingredients are evenly coated with olive oil. Pour contents of bowl on panini press, close lid, and cook for 4–6 minutes. Remove from panini press and put mixture back in bowl.

2. Scoop mixture onto the bottom halves of 4 rolls. Spread tomato sauce onto the top half of rolls. Close sandwich and place on panini press.

3. Close lid and cook for 3–5 minutes. Remove from press and slice in half. Serve warm.

2 slices honey oat bread

3 tablespoons hummus

1 small cucumber, sliced

2 slices green pepper

2 slices onion

2 leaves romaine lettuce

Veggies and Hummus Panini

This panini is a wonderful lunchtime treat for both vegetarians and meat eaters. You won't miss the cold cuts at all.

1. Preheat the panini press. On 1 slice of bread, spread the hummus and add cucumber, green pepper, onion, and lettuce. Close sandwich with another slice of bread.

2. Place on panini press, close lid, and cook for 3–5 minutes.

3. Remove from press, cut in half, and serve warm.

2 slices whole-grain bread

3 tablespoons hummus

1 celery stalk, sliced

¼ cup sprouts

Sprouts

Sprouts are highly nutritious and are usually grown from the seeds of alfalfa, mung beans, or peas. Start adding them to your panini for a healthy treat.

Hummus and Sprouts Panini

The creaminess of the hummus along with the crunch of the celery and sprouts make a great combination.

1. Preheat the panini press. On 1 slice of bread, spread the hummus and add celery and sprouts. Close sandwich with another slice of bread.

2. Place on panini press, close lid, and cook for 3–5 minutes.

3. Remove from press, cut in half, and serve warm.

½ zucchini, chopped

½ eggplant, chopped

4–6 mushrooms, sliced

2 tablespoons olive oil

2 tablespoons minced garlic

Salt and pepper, to taste

2 slices vegan whole-grain wheat bread

3 tablespoons hummus

Grilled Veggies with Hummus Panini

This is a vegan panini that's packed full of vegetables. No need for cheese or meat in this one. Check the ingredient list on your bread to make sure they didn't add any eggs or dairy to keep it vegan.

1. Preheat the panini press. Place zucchini, eggplant, and mushrooms in a bowl. Drizzle with olive oil, and add garlic, salt, and pepper. Mix well and pour contents of bowl on panini press. Close lid and cook for 3–6 minutes.

2. On 1 slice of bread, spread the hummus and add the grilled vegetables. Top with another slice of bread.

3. Place on panini press and cook for 3–5 minutes.

4. Remove from press, cut in half, and serve warm.

CHAPTER 10

Italian Favorites

Prosciutto, Onion, and Mozzarella Panini

It would be best to use a semolina peasant loaf or similar large and crusty Italian bread for this one.

1. Preheat the panini press. Place onion on panini press. Grill for 2–4 minutes and set aside.

2. On 1 slice of bread, add prosciutto, the grilled onion, and mozzarella cheese. Top with the other slice of bread.

3. Place on panini press and close the lid.

4. Cook for 3–5 minutes. Remove from press and slice in half. Serve warm.

Sausage Parmesan Panini

This panini can get messy if you overstuff it. For neater results, try slicing the sausage in half lengthwise. This will help stop it from rolling out of the panini and onto your lap.

1. Preheat the panini press. Add sausage to panini press and cook for 5–7 minutes. Remove from grill and slice in half if desired.

2. Cut open the long roll and add the sausage, mozzarella cheese, and tomato sauce.

3. Place on panini press, close lid, and cook for 2–3 minutes.

4. Cut in half and serve warm.

Caprese Panini

Caprese is a traditional Italian combination of heirloom tomatoes, buffalo mozzarella cheese, and fresh basil. It's usually served in a salad, but with the addition of a crusty ciabatta roll, you have the makings of an excellent panini.

1. Preheat the panini press. Cut ciabatta roll in half and place both pieces on counter.

2. Generously drizzle the inside of the both halves of the bread with olive oil.

3. Add mozzarella slices to the bottom of your roll. Arrange basil leaves on top of cheese. Arrange tomato on top of cheese and basil. Add salt and pepper and close sandwich. Place on panini press.

4. Close lid and cook 3–5 minutes.

5. Remove from panini press and cut in half. Serve warm.

Sandwich Options

Green, black, or Kalamata olives; roasted red peppers; and red onions are good additions to this panini. Some Italian bakeries sell bread with olives baked right in. This bread would be perfect for this sandwich.

INGREDIENTS | **SERVES 1**

1 sandwich-sized piece of baguette
1 clove garlic
4 slices tomato
2 teaspoons olive oil
1 teaspoon balsamic vinegar
Salt and pepper, to taste

Bruschetta Panini

You'll be surprised at how much flavor is transferred to the bread when you rub it with garlic. If you really love garlic, then chop up the clove when you're done with it and add it to the panini.

1. Preheat the panini press. Slice baguette lengthwise and place on panini press for about 1 minute to warm. Cut the garlic clove in half, and remove bread from press. Rub the inside of the baguette with the garlic. Add tomato slices and then drizzle with olive oil and balsamic vinegar. Add salt and pepper to taste.

2. Place baguette back on panini press, close lid, and cook for 2–4 minutes.

3. Remove from press and cut in half. Serve warm.

Cocktail Party Options

You can make this panini in bite-sized form for your next cocktail party. Use an Italian panella loaf that is sliced ¼" thick instead of the baguette. When it's done cooking, use a pizza cutter to slice into three or four pieces.

Sausage and Pepper Panini

You've probably had sausage and peppers on a long roll at an Italian fair from a street vendor, but when you seal up the ingredients in a hot panini they're even better. If you don't overstuff your panini, it'll be a lot less sloppy than the traditional sausage sandwich.

1. Preheat the panini press. Add sausage to panini press and cook for 5–7 minutes. Remove from grill and slice in half if desired.

2. Place bell peppers and onion on panini press and cook for 3–5 minutes. Remove from press and set aside.

3. Cut open the long rolls and add sausage, grilled onion and peppers, and tomato sauce on each. Place on panini press, close lid, and cook for 2–3 minutes.

4. Cut in half and serve warm.

Italian Sausage

Italian sausage comes in a two main varieties: sweet or hot. But you don't have make a decision if you don't want to. Get a little of each and mix them on your panini.

½ pound Italian pork sausage

1 cup broccoli raab

2 tablespoons olive oil

2 tablespoons minced garlic

2 long rolls

6 slices provolone cheese

Sausage and Broccoli Raab Panini

Broccoli raab is also known as broccoli rabe, broccoli di rapa, and rapini. It's a popular vegetable in southern Italian cuisine. Botanically, broccoli raab is not related to broccoli at all. Its actually a relative of the turnip.

1. Preheat the panini press. Add sausage to panini press and cook for 5–7 minutes. Remove from grill and slice in half if desired.

2. In a pot of boiling water, blanch the broccoli raab for 2–3 minutes. Remove from water and submerge in an ice bath. Drain the raab in a colander. In a bowl combine broccoli raab, olive oil, and garlic. Pour contents of bowl on panini press and cook for 3–5 minutes.

3. Cut open the long rolls and add sausage, broccoli raab, and provolone on each. Place on panini press, close lid, and cook for additional 2–3 minutes.

4. Cut in half and serve warm.

Variations

You can add some spicy heat to this panini by using hot sausage. Need even more heat? Add about a ½ teaspoon of hot pepper flakes when cooking the broccoli raab.

Sausage and Grape Panini

Sausages and grapes go together like prosciutto and figs. They're two great flavors that taste delicious together.

1. Preheat the panini press. Add sausage to panini press and cook for 5–7 minutes. Remove from grill and slice in half if desired.

2. Cut the grapes in half or give them a rough chop and put them in a bowl. Add the olive oil and balsamic vinegar and mix well.

3. Cut open the long rolls and add sausage and the grape mixture.

4. Place on panini press, close lid, and cook for 2–3 minutes.

5. Cut in half and serve warm.

Italian Sausage and Egg Panini

What better way to start your day than with some hearty Italian sausage? The fantastic scents from the kitchen should wake everyone up in your house. This panini also makes a delicious lunch.

1. Preheat the panini press. Add sausage to panini press and cook for 5–7 minutes. Remove from grill and slice in half if desired.

2. In a frying pan that has been sprayed with nonstick cooking spray, scramble or fry the eggs.

3. Cut open the long roll and add the sausages, the eggs, and the roasted red peppers.

4. Place on panini press, close lid, and cook for 2–3 minutes.

5. Cut in half and serve warm.

INGREDIENTS | SERVES 1

2 eggs

½ red bell pepper, sliced

½ onion, sliced

1 tablespoon minced garlic

2 tablespoons olive oil

Salt and pepper, to taste

¼ teaspoon hot pepper flakes

1 long roll

Pepper and Egg Panini

This is a popular sandwich in New York pizzerias that can easily be made panini style. But it isn't just for breakfast; you can enjoy it all day long.

1. In a frying pan that has been sprayed with nonstick cooking spray, scramble or fry the eggs and set aside.

2. Preheat the panini press. Place the red bell pepper and onion in a bowl. Add the garlic, olive oil, salt, pepper, and hot pepper flakes and mix well.

3. Pour contents of bowl on panini press and cook for 3–5 minutes. Cut open long roll and add the eggs and the onion and pepper.

4. Place on panini press, close lid, and cook for 2–3 minutes.

5. Cut in half and serve warm.

INGREDIENTS | SERVES 1

1 ciabatta roll
3 slices salami
3 slices prosciutto
4 slices pepperoni
3 slices provolone cheese
2 slices tomato
2 tablespoons mayonnaise

Salami, Prosciutto, and Pepperoni Panini

Italian cold cuts and cheese taste even better when warmed up inside a panini press. The melted cheese and mayonnaise is just icing on the cake.

1. Preheat the panini press. Cut open a ciabatta roll and add the salami, prosciutto, pepperoni, provolone cheese, and tomato slices. Spread mayonnaise on the other side of the roll and close the sandwich. Place on panini press.

2. Close lid and cook for 3–5 minutes, then remove from press. Cut in half and serve warm.

CHAPTER 11

Not Your Everyday Panini

8 ounces chicken broth

1 tablespoon cornstarch

1 chicken cutlet, cut into bite-sized pieces

½ cup peas

½ cup chopped carrots

½ cup chopped celery

1 onion, chopped

Salt and pepper, to taste

2 large chewy rolls

Chicken Pot Pie Panini

The key to this panini is to adjust the recipe to make it moist enough so that it isn't dry but dry enough to not fall apart. A large chewy roll will help.

1. In a small saucepan heat the chicken broth. Add corn starch and stir until fully dissolved. Add chicken to broth. Add peas, carrots, celery, onion, salt, and pepper; cover pot, and bring to boil. Reduce heat and simmer for a half hour.

2. Check consistency of the pot pie mixture. If it's too runny for a panini, let it simmer with the lid off for another 10 minutes.

3. Preheat the panini press. Cut rolls and scoop out extra bread to create a pocket. Place on panini press and spoon pot pie mixture into pocket. Add tops to rolls and close the lid.

4. Cook for 3–5 minutes. Remove from press and serve warm.

1 package frozen spinach
2 tablespoons olive oil
1 chopped onion
8 ounces feta cheese
2 tablespoons fresh parsley
6 (5" square) sheets puff pastry

Spanakopita Panini

This Greek favorite will be a lot thinner when made panini style, but it's just as tasty.

1. Cook frozen spinach according to directions on package, and drain excess water.

2. In a bowl combine the spinach, olive oil, onion, feta cheese, and parsley. Mix well. Preheat the panini press.

3. Place the puff pastry on panini press and do not close the lid. Cook for 2–4 minutes and remove. Repeat until a single side of each of the sheets is cooked. Scoop spinach mixture onto cooked sides of 3 puff pastry sheets and top with a second sheet. The uncooked side should be facing outward.

4. Place back on the panini press, close lid and cook for 3–5 minutes. Remove from press and serve warm.

Kolokithopita Panini

INGREDIENTS | SERVES 2

1 can pumpkin pie filling
1 egg
8 ounces feta cheese
2 tablespoons butter
4 (5" square) puff pastry sheets

Pumpkin pie filling isn't just for making pies. It can also be used for pumpkin panini.

1. Preheat the panini press. In a bowl combine the pumpkin pie filling, egg, feta cheese, and butter. Mix well.

2. Place puff pastry on panini press and do not close the lid. Cook for 2–4 minutes and remove. Repeat until single side of each of the sheets is grilled. Scoop pumpkin mixture onto cooked sides of 2 puff pastry sheets and top with a second sheet. The uncooked sides should be facing outward.

3. Place back on the panini press, close lid, and cook for 3–5 minutes. Remove from press and serve warm.

Variations

You can also add chopped walnuts and cinnamon to make the Kolokithopita Panini sweeter.

¼ cup lime juice

2 tablespoons chopped garlic

1 tablespoon cilantro

2 tablespoons olive oil

1 teaspoon cumin

1 pound flank steak

1 onion, sliced

1 bell pepper, sliced

4 flour tortillas

2 tablespoons Salsa (see Chapter 19)

2 tablespoons Guacamole (see Chapter 19)

Steak Fajita Panini

You can go a few different ways with your bread selection for this panini. A flour tortilla is traditional, but you may also like French bread or even a sourdough loaf.

1. In a container large enough to hold the steak, combine lime juice, garlic, cilantro, olive oil, and cumin and mix well. Lay the steak in the container and marinate for at least 1 hour.

2. Preheat the panini press. Place the steak on panini press, close lid, and cook for 5–6 minutes or until the steak reaches an internal temperature of 125°F (medium rare). Remove from press and let cool for 5 minutes, then cut into slices.

3. Place onion and pepper on panini press. Close lid and grill for 2–4 minutes and set aside.

4. On a flour tortilla, add steak, grilled onion and pepper, Salsa, and Guacamole. Fold tortilla into half-moon shape and place on panini press. Use this process to assemble panini for the remaining 3 tortillas.

5. Cook each panini for 3–5 minutes. Remove from press and cut with pizza cutter. Serve warm with extra Salsa and sour cream.

Marinating Steak

If you buy your steak in bulk at big box stores, you probably have to split the package into a few smaller portions for freezing. When you do that, it's a great time to add your marinade. When the meat freezes and then thaws, it really soaks up the marinade.

¼ cup lime juice

2 tablespoons chopped garlic

1 tablespoon cilantro

2 tablespoons olive oil

1 teaspoon cumin

1 pound thin-sliced chicken cutlets

1 onion, sliced

1 bell pepper, sliced

6 slices bread

2 tablespoons Salsa (see Chapter 19)

2 tablespoons Guacamole (see Chapter 19)

Chicken Fajita Panini

Chicken fajitas are just as tasty when you make them on crusty bread. A Cheddar jalapeño loaf is a great bread choice for this panini.

1. In a container large enough to hold the chicken, combine the lime juice, garlic, cilantro, olive oil, and cumin and mix well. Lay the chicken in the container and marinate for at least 1 hour.

2. Preheat the panini press. Place the chicken cutlets on panini press, close lid, and cook for 3–5 minutes. The cooking time will depend on the thickness of the cutlets. Remove from press and let cool for 5 minutes, then cut into slices.

3. Place onion and pepper on panini press. Close lid and grill for 2–4 minutes; set aside.

4. On 3 slices of bread, add chicken, grilled onion and pepper, salsa, and guacamole. Close sandwiches with remaining 3 slices of bread and place on panini press.

5. Close lid and cook for 3–5 minutes. Remove from press and cut in half. Serve warm with extra Salsa and sour cream.

Variations

Additional items to try on your fajita panini would be cheese, sour cream, or chili peppers. Poblano Chili Sauce (see Chapter 19) and cooked brown rice can also be added.

¼ cup lime juice

2 tablespoons minced garlic

1 tablespoon cilantro

2 tablespoons olive oil

1 teaspoon cumin

1 pound medium shrimp, peeled and deveined

1 onion, sliced

1 bell pepper, sliced

4 flour tortillas

2 tablespoons Salsa (see Chapter 19)

3 tablespoons black beans

2 tablespoons Guacamole (see Chapter 19)

Shrimp Fajita Panini

Shrimp or scallops can be used to make a fajita panini from the sea.

1. In a bowl, combine the lime juice, garlic, cilantro, olive oil, and cumin and mix well. Lay the shrimp in the container and marinate for about 5 minutes.

2. Preheat the panini press. Place the shrimp on panini press, close lid, and cook for 2–3 minutes. Remove from press and set aside.

3. Place onion and pepper on panini press. Close lid and grill for 2–4 minutes; set aside.

4. On each flour tortilla, add shrimp, grilled onion and pepper, Salsa, black beans, and Guacamole. Fold tortillas into half-moon shapes and place on panini press.

5. Close lid and cook for 3–5 minutes. Remove from press and cut with pizza cutter. Serve warm with extra Salsa and sour cream.

Seafood Fajitas

Other seafoods can be used besides shrimp or scallops. Try it using swordfish, tuna, or even tilapia.

INGREDIENTS | SERVES 1

2 slices Italian bread
½ pound sliced lamb (cooked)
4 tablespoons baba ganoush
¼ cup feta cheese

Lamb, Baba Ganoush, and Feta Panini

This panini is great when you have leftover roasted lamb shoulder or lamb chops on hand. If you don't, you can sometimes find lamb cubes for stew at your supermarket's butcher's department that will work nicely, too.

1. Preheat the panini press. On 1 slice of bread, arrange the lamb slices and scoop on the baba ganoush. Sprinkle the feta cheese on top and close sandwich with the other slice of bread.

2. Place on panini press and close the lid.

3. Cook for 3–5 minutes. Remove from press and slice in half. Serve warm.

Baba Ganoush

Baba ganoush is a popular Middle Eastern dish that's made from eggplant. It's often eaten with warm pitas and used for dunking, but it can also be used as a sauce or spread, as it is on this panini.

Sardine and Arugula Panini

Sardines are full of protein and loaded with omega-3 fatty acids. Plus, they're usually packed in heart-healthy olive oil. Just be sure to watch the sodium.

1. Preheat the panini press. On 1 slice of bread, arrange the sardines, onion, and tomato and top with a handful of arugula. Shred the arugula if desired.

2. Spread the mayonnaise on the other slice of bread and top sandwich.

3. Place on panini press and close the lid.

4. Cook for 3–5 minutes. Remove from press and slice in half. Serve warm.

Sardines and Mercury

Sardines contain lower amounts of mercury and other toxins than most other fish, which makes them an ideal choice for pregnant women and children.

2 hard-boiled eggs, peeled

2 slices Italian bread

6–9 anchovies in oil

2 tablespoons capers

3 tablespoons mayonnaise

Salt and pepper, to taste

Hard-Boiled Egg with Anchovy Panini

The exact time it takes to hard-boil an egg depends on the size of the egg, the amount of water used, and the altitude of the cooking location. Leave them in the water for 10–15 minutes after they cook to ensure that they're fully hard-boiled.

1. Preheat the panini press. Slice 2 hard-boiled eggs and lay the slices on 1 slice of bread. Add the anchovies and the capers.

2. Spread mayonnaise on the other slice of bread, add salt and pepper to taste, and top sandwich.

3. Place on press and close the lid.

4. Cook for 3–5 minutes. Remove from press and slice in half. Serve warm.

INGREDIENTS | **SERVES 2**

2 tablespoons minced garlic

2 tablespoons peanut oil

10–12 medium shrimp, peeled and deveined

2 long rolls

½–1 cup shredded romaine lettuce

3 slices tomato

2 tablespoons Creole Mayonnaise (see Chapter 19)

Grilled Po' Boy Panini

This po' boy sandwich is so poor that it can't even afford the bread crumbs that are usually used to coat the shrimp! Grilling shrimp is healthier than deep-frying, and it'll also be much easier to clean up your panini press when you are done.

1. Preheat the panini press. In a bowl combine the garlic, peanut oil, and shrimp and mix until evenly coated.

2. Pour contents of bowl on panini press, close lid, and cook for 2–3 minutes. Remove from press and set aside.

3. Cut 2 long rolls in half and add the shrimp, romaine lettuce, and tomato. Spread Creole Mayonnaise on the lid of each roll and place on top of sandwiches.

4. Place on panini press and close the lid. Cook for 3–5 minutes. Remove from press and slice sandwiches in half. Serve warm.

2 tablespoons minced garlic

1 teaspoon hot pepper flakes

2 tablespoons olive oil

10–12 medium shrimp, peeled and deveined

2 long rolls

2 slices red pepper

3 slices onion

5–6 slices jalapeño peppers

2 tablespoons Creole Mayonnaise (see Chapter 19)

Spicy Po' Boy Panini

This is the po' boy that adds the heat. If jalapeño peppers are too tame for you, then break out the habaneros.

1. Preheat the panini press. In a bowl combine the garlic, hot pepper flakes, olive oil, and shrimp and mix until evenly coated.

2. Pour contents of bowl on panini press, close lid, and cook for 2–3 minutes. Remove from press and set aside.

3. Cut long rolls in half and add the shrimp, red pepper, onion, and jalapeño pepper slices. Spread Creole Mayonnaise on the lids of the rolls and place on top of sandwiches.

4. Place on panini press and close the lid. Cook for 3–5 minutes. Remove from press and slice sandwiches in half. Serve warm.

4 slices baloney

2 slices corn bread

4 slices Cheddar cheese

Fried Baloney and Cheese on Corn Bread

This recipe may sound a little odd, but something about the combination of flavors really works. Give it a try before you judge it.

1. Preheat the panini press. Fry the baloney slices on the press for 2–3 minutes and set aside.

2. On 1 slice of corn bread, add the fried baloney and the Cheddar cheese. Close the sandwich with the other slice of corn bread.

3. Place on the panini press and close the lid.

4. Cook for 3–5 minutes. Remove from press and slice in half. Serve warm.

Variations

Butter or mayonnaise will keep this panini from getting too dry. Add a few jalapeño pepper slices to give it a little more bite.

1–2 chicken cutlets, sliced in bite-sized pieces

3 tablespoons canola oil

2 tablespoons minced garlic

1 teaspoon grated ginger

1 tablespoon curry paste

2 slices naan

¼ cup grated carrot

1 cup shredded mixed greens

Curried Chicken Panini

Curry can be overpowering if you're not used to it. Don't let the chicken marinate as long if you're a curry newbie.

1. Add chicken to a bowl with canola oil, garlic, ginger, and curry paste and mix well. Marinate for 10 minutes. Preheat the panini press. Pour contents of bowl on panini press, close lid, and cook for 4–6 minutes. Remove from press and let cool.

2. On 1 slice of bread add the cooked chicken, grated carrot, and mixed greens. Add another slice of bread on top and place on panini press.

3. Close lid and cook for 3–5 minutes. Remove from press and slice in half. Serve warm.

Naan

Naan is a soft flatbread that is popular in Southern Asian countries. It is usually larger than a pita and is great to use for panini.

Inside Out Grilled Chicken, Bacon, and Cheese Panini

Fast-food chicken restaurants offer this breadless sandwich with a fried crispy chicken patty to serve as the bun. Why not make it a tiny bit healthier with grilled chicken?

1. Preheat the panini press. Cook bacon on panini press until crisp and set aside.

2. Place chicken cutlets on press, close lid, and cook for 3–5 minutes. Open press and lay the bacon and cheese on one chicken cutlet and spread the mayonnaise on the other one. Carefully flip the mayonnaise-covered cutlet on top of the bacon-and-cheese-covered one.

3. Close press and cook for an additional 1–2 minutes.

4. Remove from press and wrap in a paper towel or napkin and serve hot.

Jalapeño Popper Panini

All peppers are delicious on sandwiches when you grill them. Leave off the breading for these jalapeño poppers when you make them panini style.

1. Preheat the panini press. Place the jalapeño peppers on panini press and close lid. Cook for 3–5 minutes. Remove from press and place on a cutting board. Scrape off any black char marks and cut into slices. Remove seeds and stems.

2. Arrange the roasted jalapeños onto 1 slice of bread and top with Cheddar cheese. Close sandwich with another slice of bread and place on panini press, close lid, and cook for 2–4 minutes.

3. Remove from press and cut in half. Serve warm.

Variations

All of your favorite jalapeño popper variations will work with this jalapeño popper panini. Be sure to try this recipe with bacon or andouille sausage. Also, you could substitute the Cheddar cheese with a mixture of cream cheese and Monterey jack cheese.

Turkey Taco Panini

INGREDIENTS | SERVES 1

2 slices bread
4 slices cooked turkey breast
3 slices Monterey jack cheese
3 slices avocado
2 tablespoons cranberry salsa

If there was such thing as a Thanksgiving taco, this panini would be its cousin. Onion bread or even pumpernickel are both good choices for this one.

1. Preheat the panini press. On 1 slice of bread, add turkey, cheese, avocado, and salsa. Top with another slice of bread.

2. Place on panini press and close the lid.

3. Cook for 3–5 minutes. Remove from press and slice in half. Serve warm.

Chili Dog Panini

INGREDIENTS | SERVES 1

2 hot dogs
1 hard roll
3 tablespoons chili

Variations

Cheddar cheese always goes well with chili. Add a little bit before closing the panini. Jalapeño peppers and sour cream can be added too. Or, if you can find good hearty corn bread, skip the hard roll and use that instead.

This is a great solution to the question of what to do with leftover chili. Use a big hearty roll to hold the chili inside the panini.

1. Preheat the panini press. Cook hot dogs on panini press for 3–5 minutes and set aside.

2. Cut open a hard roll and scoop out some bread to form a pocket. Add the hot dogs and the chili and close roll.

3. Place on panini press, close lid, and cook for 2–4 minutes. Remove from press and serve warm.

2 hot dogs

1 hard roll

1 tablespoon mustard

1 tablespoon relish

2 tablespoons chopped grilled onions

Hot Dog with the Works Panini

Once you get a taste for hot dogs on good quality bread, you'll say goodbye to those boring hot dog rolls.

1. Preheat the panini press. Cook hot dogs on panini press for 3–5 minutes and set aside.

2. Cut open a hard roll and scoop out some bread to form a pocket. Add the hot dogs, mustard, relish, and grilled onions and close roll. Place on panini press.

3. Close lid and cook for 2–4 minutes and remove from press. Serve warm.

Variations

There are so many hot dog variations that you can try when you make them panini style. Be sure to try one or more of the following: ketchup, chili, sauerkraut, relish, mustard, or baked beans. The hard roll really keeps it all together neatly, so load up on your favorites.

INGREDIENTS | SERVES 1

2 hot dogs

1 hard roll

2 tablespoons mustard

3 tablespoons sauerkraut

Hot Dog and Sauerkraut Panini

The basic hot dog that you get at a ballpark is so good when made panini style that you'll be annoyed that there aren't more panini presses at baseball games.

1. Preheat the panini press. Cook hot dogs on panini press for 3–5 minutes and set aside.

2. Cut open a hard roll and scoop out some bread to form a pocket. Add the hot dogs, mustard, and sauerkraut and close roll. Place on panini press.

3. Close lid and cook for 2–4 minutes and remove from press. Serve warm.

Slicing Hot Dogs

You have a few choices when adding hot dogs to a panini. You can put them in whole, slice them into bite-sized pieces, or slice them lengthwise. Make your decision based on your choice of bread. Thicker bread can handle thicker hot dog pieces.

3 strips bacon

5–7 white mushrooms, sliced

2 tablespoons olive oil

Salt and pepper, to taste

2 slices Italian bread

¼ cup chopped Kalamata olives

1 teaspoon Worcestershire sauce

1 tablespoon Parmesan cheese

Mushroom, Bacon, and Olive Panini

Kalamata is a region of Greece that's famous for its olives. Kalamata olives are great on panini sandwiches no matter where you live.

1. Preheat the panini press. Cook bacon on panini press until crisp and set aside.

2. Place the mushrooms on the panini press. Drizzle with olive oil and sprinkle with salt and pepper. Close lid and cook for 3–5 minutes, then set aside.

3. On 1 slice of bread add the mushrooms, Kalamata olives, Worcestershire sauce, and Parmesan cheese; top with the other slice of bread.

4. Place on panini press, close lid, and cook for 2–4 minutes.

5. Remove from press and cut in half. Serve warm.

CHAPTER 12

Dunk That Panini

1 egg
½ cup milk
1 teaspoon cinnamon
2 slices bread
3 slices ham
3 slices cooked turkey breast
3 slices Swiss cheese
Powdered sugar, to taste
½ cup maple syrup

Monte Cristo

The Monte Cristo sandwich is usually served with fresh fruit, fruit preserves, warm maple syrup, or powdered sugar. This panini version can be served with all of those options. Challah or another sweet bread will taste best.

1. In a flat bowl or any other container that will fit 1 slice of bread, add egg, milk, and cinnamon. Mix well with a whisk.

2. Preheat the panini press. On a slice of bread add the ham, turkey, and Swiss cheese and top sandwich with another slice of bread.

3. Dunk entire sandwich into milk and egg mixture and coat both sides. Place on panini press and close the lid.

4. Cook for 3–5 minutes.

5. Remove from panini press and cut in half. Sprinkle with powdered sugar and serve warm with maple syrup for dunking.

Variation

For a firmer panini, toast the bread before dunking it in the French toast batter.

INGREDIENTS | SERVES 1

1 hamburger patty

1 egg

½ cup milk

1 teaspoon cinnamon

2 slices challah bread

3 slices ham

3 slices cooked turkey breast

3 slices Swiss cheese

¼ cup maple syrup

Monte Cristo Burger

French toast can make any meal a happy one. This burger may not be on the diet menu, but it's worth the splurge.

1. Preheat the panini press. Place hamburger patty on panini press. If your press has a drip spout for excess grease to run off, you'll want to put a small container underneath. Cook 3–4 minutes, less if a rare burger is desired. Remove cooked burger and set aside.

2. Wearing an oven mitt, wipe burger grease from panini press with a wad of paper towels.

3. In a flat bowl, add egg, milk, and cinnamon. Mix well with a whisk. On a slice of bread, add the burger, ham, turkey, and cheese, and place the second slice of bread on top. Dunk the entire sandwich into the milk and egg mixture. You will have to flip it over to coat both sides. Place on panini press and close lid.

4. Cook for 3–5 minutes and remove from press.

5. Cut in half and serve warm with maple syrup for dunking.

Variations
If making the hamburger patties from scratch, add a few tablespoons of maple syrup in the ground beef.

1 long roll
4 slices roast beef
3 slices Swiss cheese
2 slices onion
1 cup beef broth
2 teaspoons Worcestershire sauce

Roast Beef Au Jus

Au jus means "with juice," but most roast beef au jus or French dip sandwiches are served with beef broth. This panini version is much easier to dunk.

1. Preheat the panini press. Cut roll in half lengthwise and add the roast beef, Swiss cheese, and onion slices. Close sandwich and place on panini press.

2. Close lid and cook for 3–5 minutes. While it cooks, pour the beef broth in a small saucepan over medium heat and stir in the Worcestershire sauce.

3. Remove sandwich from panini press and cut in half. Serve warm with a small bowl of the warm beef broth for dunking.

Variations

Provolone cheese can be substituted for the Swiss cheese, and grilled onions make a nice addition too.

Chicken Satay Panini

The Satay Sauce (see Chapter 19) is so delicious that you may forget about the bread and eat all of the chicken before the panini press even has a chance to warm up. But when you put it all together, you'll find that it's worth the wait.

1. Preheat the panini press. Place chicken cutlets on panini press. Sprinkle with salt and pepper before closing lid. Cook for 4–6 minutes, depending on thickness of the chicken breast. Remove from panini press and set aside.

2. On 1 slice of bread, add the chicken (slice if desired) and the onion and top with another slice of bread.

3. Place on panini press, close lid, and cook for 3–5 minutes.

4. Remove from panini press and cut in half. Serve warm with a small bowl of the Satay Sauce for dunking.

Variation
The Satay Sauce can also be used as a marinade. Pour it over the chicken and let it marinate in the refrigerator for a few hours before making this recipe.

INGREDIENTS | **SERVES 1**

4 ounce filet mignon
1 long roll
1 cup béarnaise sauce

Filet Mignon and Béarnaise Dipping Sauce

Filet mignon is always great, but when you can dunk it in a bowl of béarnaise sauce it's even better. Try it with a ciabatta roll to soak up the sauce.

1. Preheat the panini press. Cook filet mignon on panini press to desired doneness and set aside to rest. Slice thinly.

2. Cut a long roll in half lengthwise and add the filet mignon slices. Place on panini press.

3. Close lid and cook for 2–3 minutes or until the bread is crispy.

4. Remove from panini press and cut in half. Serve warm with a small bowl of béarnaise sauce for dunking.

Filet Mignon

Cooking a filet mignon is a little tricky on a panini press because of its thickness. If you're new to panini grilling, it might be best to use your barbecue to cook it just right. Or, replace it with a more panini-friendly cut of beef. Use your own judgment to make the best panini possible.

Buffalo Chicken and Blue Cheese Dipping Sauce

Don't skimp on the hot sauce for this panini. The blue cheese dressing will bail you out.

1. Preheat the panini press. Place chicken cutlets on panini press. Sprinkle with salt and pepper before closing lid. Cook for 4–6 minutes, depending on thickness of the chicken breast. Remove from panini press and set aside.

2. Cut chicken into small pieces and place in a bowl with the butter and hot sauce. If the chicken is still warm the butter will melt on its own; otherwise, melt butter in the microwave first.

3. Cut a long roll in half lengthwise and pour the contents of the bowl in it.

4. Place on the panini press and close lid. Cook for 3–5 minutes.

5. Remove panini from press, cut in half, and serve warm with a bowl of blue cheese dressing for dunking.

Variations

If you're a fan of buffalo chicken salad, add some romaine lettuce to the panini. It's a panini and salad in one.

2 sweet potatoes

¾ cup sour cream

⅓ cup brown sugar

¼ cup crushed pineapple

Sweet Potato Fries with Dipping Sauce

Sweet potato fries tend to be much more moist than regular potato fries. You can blanch them or follow the cold water bath instructions below to avoid soggy fries.

1. Peel and cut the sweet potatoes into French fry shapes and place in a bowl of cold water for 30 minutes.

2. Preheat the panini press. Drain the fries and pat them dry with some paper towels. Place on panini press. Close lid and cook for about 15 minutes or until tender and crisp.

3. In a bowl combine the sour cream, brown sugar, and crushed pineapple and mix well.

4. Remove fries from panini press and serve warm with sour cream mixture for dunking.

Variations

Sweet potato fries are also good with garlic-infused oil for a dipping sauce.

½ cup bread crumbs

½ cup flaked coconut

2 eggs

8–14 jumbo shrimp, peeled and deveined

¼ cup olive oil

⅔ cup orange marmalade

2 teaspoons Dijon mustard

1 teaspoon horseradish

Coconut Shrimp with Spicy Dipping Sauce

Cooking breaded shrimp in a panini press may create odd-looking ridges on the shrimp, but it's much healthier than deep-frying them in hot oil.

1. In a bowl combine the bread crumbs and coconut and mix well. In another bowl beat eggs. Dip shrimp into eggs and then into bread crumb mixture to bread them.

2. Place breaded shrimp on a preheated panini press, close lid, and cook for 2–4 minutes.

3. In another bowl add the olive oil, marmalade, mustard, and horseradish and mix well.

4. Remove shrimp from panini press and serve warm with a bowl of the dipping sauce for dunking.

Grilled Artichokes and Sesame Dipping Sauce

Toasted sesame oil has a unique nutty flavor that can give any almost any dish a nice Asian flair. You'll want to use a big bowl for your dipping sauce.

1. On 1 slice of bread add the artichoke hearts and top sandwich with another slice of bread. Place on panini press, close lid, and cook for 3–5 minutes.

2. In a bowl combine the rest of the ingredients and mix well.

3. Remove panini from press, cut in half, and serve warm with a bowl of the soy sauce mixture for dunking.

Sweet and Sour Chicken

Plain chicken breast is quite tasty when dunked in sweet and sour sauce.

1. Preheat the panini press. Place chicken cutlets on panini press. Sprinkle with salt and pepper before closing lid. Cook for 4–6 minutes, depending on thickness of the chicken breast. Remove from panini press and set aside.

2. Cut chicken cutlets into strips and serve with sweet and sour sauce for dunking.

Bread Sticks

Good quality pizza dough is the key to these odd-looking but delicious bread sticks.

INGREDIENTS | SERVES 2

2 cups pizza dough
1 tablespoon olive oil
1 cup tomato sauce

Variation

If your panini press has a nonridged set of metal cooking plates, you may want to use them to make ridgeless bread sticks.

1. Preheat the panini press. Knead and roll out pizza dough. Cut dough into 1½" strips.

2. Place dough strips on panini press and drizzle with olive oil, then close lid and cook for 3–5 minutes.

3. Remove from press and serve warm with tomato sauce for dunking.

Onion and Mozzarella Panini

Plan on staying home after eating this onion panini on an onion roll. It tastes so good that you probably won't mind a night alone.

INGREDIENTS | SERVES 1

1 onion, sliced
1 onion roll
4 slices mozzarella cheese
1 cup tomato sauce

Simple Panini

The panini that you see at upscale cafes usually consist of five or more ingredients. That's great, but sometimes it's easier to take a few of your favorites and eat a simple panini. For example, in this recipe, there is onion, cheese, and tomato sauce, and that's plenty.

1. Preheat the panini press. Place onion on panini press. Close lid and cook for 3–5 minutes.

2. Cut open an onion roll and add the mozzarella cheese and the grilled onions. Close the roll and place on panini press.

3. Close lid and cook for 3–5 minutes. Remove from press, cut in half, and serve warm with tomato sauce for dunking.

1 eggplant, peeled and diced
1 tomato, chopped
1 onion, chopped
4 cloves garlic
3 tablespoons lemon juice
2 tablespoons tahini
1 tablespoon olive oil
4 tablespoons water
4 pitas

Grilled Eggplant Dip with Warm Pita Bread

The panini press does double duty with this recipe by grilling the vegetables and then heating up the pita bread.

1. Preheat the panini press. Place eggplant on panini press, close lid, and cook for 3–5 minutes. Remove from press and place in a food processor. Add the tomato, onion, garlic, lemon juice, tahini, and olive oil into the food processor and chop until well blended. Slowly add water and blend until desired consistency is reached. Empty into a serving dish.

2. Use the panini press to warm up the pitas for about 1 minute, and then cut pitas into quarters.

3. Serve warmed pita slices with the eggplant mixture for dipping.

CHAPTER 13

Cocktail Party Panini

8–12 medium shrimp, peeled and deveined

8 ounces artichoke hearts

1 cup mayonnaise

1 cup Parmesan cheese

½ teaspoon garlic powder

12 slices Italian panella bread sliced ¼" thick

Shrimp and Artichoke Dip Panini

When you aren't making a panini sandwich with your panini press, you can use it to grill shrimp quickly and easily.

1. Preheat the panini press. Place the shrimp on panini press, close lid, and cook for 3–5 minutes. Remove from grill and set aside.

2. Place the artichoke hearts on the panini press, close lid, and cook for 3–5 minutes. Remove from grill and set aside.

3. Combine all ingredients except bread in a food processor and give them a rough chop.

4. Divide mixture onto 6 slices of bread, cover with remaining 6 slices, and place on panini grill. Close lid and cook for 2–4 minutes or until the bread is crispy.

5. Remove from press and place on a cutting board. Use a pizza cutter to cut each sandwich into about four bite-sized pieces. Serve warm.

1 package frozen spinach
1 3-ounce package cream cheese
1 cup mayonnaise
1 teaspoon garlic powder
1 cup Parmesan cheese
Salt and pepper, to taste
8 thin slices Italian bread

Parmesan Spinach Panini

Thin-sliced Italian bread is the best bread option for cocktail parties. Save the Kaiser rolls for a burger. Party snacks should be easy to hold.

1. Cook the frozen spinach in the microwave according to instructions on the package and then drain as much water from it as you can.

2. Combine all ingredients except for bread in a food processor and give them a rough chop. Preheat the panini press.

3. Divide mixture onto 4 slices of bread and top with remaining slices. Place on panini grill, close lid, and cook for 2–4 minutes or until the bread is crispy.

4. Remove from press and place on a cutting board. Use a pizza cutter to cut each panini into four bite-sized pieces. Serve warm.

4–8 crimini mushrooms, sliced

1 cup crabmeat

1 cup cream cheese

4 tablespoons Parmesan cheese

1 teaspoon fresh parsley

2 tablespoons seasoned bread crumbs

8 slices Italian panella bread, sliced ¼" thick

Mushroom and Crabmeat Panini

Use a pizza cutter to cut these panini into bite-sized pieces for your guests.

1. Preheat the panini press. Place the mushrooms on the panini press, close lid, and cook for 2–4 minutes. Remove from grill and set aside.

2. Combine all ingredients except for bread in a food processor and give them a rough chop.

3. Divide mixture between 4 slices of bread and top with remaining slices. Place on panini grill, close lid, and cook for 2–4 minutes or until the bread is crispy.

4. Remove from press and place on a cutting board. Use a pizza cutter to cut each panini into four bite-sized pieces. Serve warm.

INGREDIENTS | SERVES 4

6 tablespoons ricotta cheese

4 slices Italian panella bread, sliced ¼"
thick

½ cup sun-dried tomatoes in oil

Sun-Dried Tomato and Ricotta Panini

Use a light touch with the ricotta cheese so that it doesn't squirt out in your panini maker. Nothing stops a party quicker than the smell of burnt cheese.

1. Preheat the panini press. Spread the ricotta cheese on 2 slices of bread, and place the sun-dried tomatoes on top. Close the sandwiches with the remaining two slices of bread. Place on panini grill, close lid, and cook for 2–4 minutes or until the bread is crispy.

2. Remove from press and place on a cutting board. Use a pizza cutter to cut each panini into four bite-sized pieces. Serve warm.

INGREDIENTS | SERVES 4

8 (5" square) puff pastry sheets

1 cup Cheddar cheese

Cheese Puff Panini

These are very easy to make, but your guests will think that you hired a caterer.

1. Preheat the panini press. Place the pastry sheets on panini press and leave the lid open. Cook for 2–3 minutes, then remove from press.

2. Place the Cheddar cheese onto the cooked sides of 4 sheets of puff pastry. Cover with remaining 4 sheets, with the cooked sides facing in. Return to panini press, close lid, and cook for 2–4 minutes.

3. Remove from press and place on a cutting board. Use a pizza cutter to cut each panini into four bite-sized pieces. Serve warm.

INGREDIENTS | SERVES 4

8 (5" square) puff pastry sheets

3 slices provolone cheese

1 tablespoon Pesto Sauce (see Chapter 19)

Cheese Pesto Puff Panini

Cheese puffs are party favorites. You should also offer the Italian version for some variety.

1. Preheat the panini press. Place the pastry sheets on panini press and leave the lid open. Cook for 2–3 minutes, then remove from press.

2. Place the provolone cheese and pesto onto the cooked sides of 4 sheets of puff pastry. Cover with remaining 4 sheets, with the cooked sides facing in. Return to panini press, close lid, and cook for 2–4 minutes.

3. Remove from press and place on a cutting board. Use a pizza cutter to cut each panini into four bite-sized pieces. Serve warm.

Cooking in Advance

Make these panini before your party guests arrive, let them cool a little and then place them in a lasagna pan. You should reheat at low temperature (300°F) during the party. Don't let them get too hot or else they'll melt into a giant pan-shaped ball of cheese.

INGREDIENTS | SERVES 4

10 strips bacon

10–15 medium shrimp, peeled and deveined

2 tablespoons olive oil

1 teaspoon minced garlic

2 slices Italian panella bread, sliced ¼" thick

Bacon and Shrimp Panini

Bacon-wrapped shrimp is common at cocktail parties, but who has time to wrap anything? Put the shrimp and bacon between some thin-sliced bread and let your panini press do the wrapping.

1. Cook bacon on panini press until crisp. Remove and set aside.

2. Place the shrimp in a bowl with the olive oil and the garlic and mix to coat evenly. Empty contents of bowl on a preheated panini press, close lid, and cook for 3–5 minutes. Remove from grill and set aside.

3. Arrange the shrimp and the bacon between 2 slices of bread and place on panini grill. Close lid and cook for an additional 2–4 minutes or until the bread is crispy.

4. Remove from press and place on a cutting board. Use a pizza cutter to cut each panini into four bite-sized pieces. Serve warm.

Pork Satay

INGREDIENTS | SERVES 4

2 boneless pork chops, cut into ½"
pieces
¼ cup Satay Sauce (see Chapter 19)
2 slices Italian panella bread, sliced
¼" thick

*You can also make this pork satay shish kebab style and
serve it with the Satay Sauce for dipping.*

1. Place pork in a bowl and pour the Satay Sauce
   over it. Marinate for at least 30 minutes.

2. Preheat the panini press. Place contents of bowl
   on panini press. Close lid and cook for 4–6
   minutes.

3. Put the cooked pork between 2 slices of bread and
   return to panini press to cook for an additional 2–4
   minutes.

4. Remove from press and place on a cutting board.
   Use a pizza cutter to cut each panini into four bite-
   sized pieces. Serve warm.

Pear, Goat Cheese, and Pancetta Panini

INGREDIENTS | SERVES 1

3 thin slices pancetta
4 slices pear
2 slices crusty Italian bread
3 tablespoons goat cheese
1 teaspoon honey

*Pancetta is a dry cured meat that is similar to bacon.
And just like bacon, it goes great with a lot of different
ingredients, including fruit. You'll definitely want a crusty
Italian bread for this panini.*

1. Preheat the panini press. Cook pancetta on panini
   press until crisp and set aside.

2. Lay pear slices on a slice of bread. Add the
   pancetta and goat cheese and then drizzle with
   honey. Top with another slice of bread.

3. Place it on the panini press. Close the lid and cook
   for 2–3 minutes or until bread is crispy.

4. Remove from press and slice in half. Serve warm.

Prosciutto and Asparagus Panini

INGREDIENTS | SERVES 1

10 thin asparagus spears
2 tablespoons olive oil
4 slices prosciutto
2 slices provolone cheese
2 slices Italian panella bread, sliced ¼" thick

Find the thinnest asparagus spears that you can. You can also use a vegetable peeler to make the stalks a little thinner if you need to.

1. Preheat the panini press. Place asparagus on panini press and drizzle with olive oil. Close lid and cook for 2–4 minutes, then remove from press.

2. Arrange the asparagus, the prosciutto, and the provolone cheese between 2 slices of bread. Place on the panini grill, close lid, and cook for 2–4 minutes or until the bread is crispy.

3. Remove from press and place on a cutting board. Use a pizza cutter to cut each panini into four bite-sized pieces. Serve warm.

Gruyère with Chives Pastry Dippers

INGREDIENTS | SERVES 1

2 puff pastry sheets
4 slices Gruyère cheese
1 tablespoon chopped chives
½ cup sour cream

Gruyère tends to be expensive, so use regular Swiss if you want. You'll still have a tasty panini.

1. Preheat the panini press. Place the puff pastry on panini press and do not close the lid. Cook for 2–4 minutes and remove. Lay Gruyère cheese and chives onto the cooked sides of 2 puff pastry sheets. Add the other puff pastry sheets on top with the cooked sides facing inward.

2. Place on panini press, close lid, and cook for 3–5 minutes. Remove from press and slice in half. Serve warm with side of sour cream.

INGREDIENTS | SERVES 4

4 puff pastry sheets
8 ounces smoked salmon
1 cup sour cream
1 tablespoon horseradish
1 tablespoon capers
1 chopped shallot
1 tablespoon butter

Salmon Puff Panini

Presentation is everything, so be sure to put a neat little dollop of sour cream on top of these before serving.

1. Preheat the panini press. Place the pastry sheets on panini press and leave the lid open. Cook for 2–3 minutes, then remove from press.

2. Mix the rest of the ingredients in a bowl, and spread the mixture on the cooked sides of 2 pastry sheets. Cover the mixture with the cooked sides of the remaining two pastry sheets. Place on the panini grill, close lid, and cook for 2–4 minutes.

3. Remove from press and place on a cutting board. Use a pizza cutter to cut each panini into four bite-sized pieces. Serve warm.

Salmon and Mushroom Puff Panini

Crimini mushrooms add a nice earthy flavor to these salmon puffs. Use chopped portobello mushrooms if you can't find any crimini.

1. Preheat the panini press. Place the pastry sheets on panini press and leave the lid open. Cook for 2–3 minutes, then remove from press and set aside.

2. Place salmon fillet on the panini press and drizzle with olive oil. Close lid and cook for 4–6 minutes, then set aside.

3. Place butter in a frying pan and add mushrooms, shallot, and thyme and sauté for 2–3 minutes.

4. Spoon mushroom mixture onto cooked side of 4 pastry sheets, then divide salmon into quarters and add on top. Close sandwiches with another pastry sheet with the cooked side facing inside. Return to panini press, close lid, and cook for an additional 1–2 minutes.

5. Remove from press and place on a cutting board. Use a pizza cutter to cut each panini into four bite-sized pieces. Serve warm.

INGREDIENTS | SERVES 4

8 (5" square) puff pastry sheets
1 (8-ounce) salmon fillet
2 tablespoons olive oil
2 tablespoons butter
1 chopped shallot
½ teaspoon thyme
½ teaspoon parsley
1 cup spinach

Salmon and Spinach Puff Panini

Go easy on the fillings for these puff panini. Appetizers are meant to get you ready for dinner, not fill you up.

1. Preheat the panini press. Place the pastry sheets on a preheated panini press and leave the lid open. Cook for 2–3 minutes, then remove from press and set aside.

2. Place salmon fillets on the panini press and drizzle with olive oil. Close lid and cook for 4–6 minutes, then set aside.

3. Place butter in a frying pan and add shallot, thyme, and parsley and sauté for 1–2 minutes. Add spinach to the pan and cook until spinach is wilted.

4. Spoon spinach mixture onto cooked side of 4 pastry sheets, then divide salmon into quarters and add on top. Close sandwich with another pastry sheet with the cooked side facing inside. Return to panini press, close lid, and cook for an additional 1–2 minutes.

5. Remove from press and place on a cutting board. Use a pizza cutter to cut each panini into four bite-sized pieces. Serve warm.

½ pound ground beef
1 egg
1 cup bread crumbs
1 chopped onion
3 tablespoons milk
1 tablespoon ketchup
½ cup grated Parmesan cheese
Salt and pepper, to taste
8 (5" square) puff pastry sheets

Meatball Puff Panini

This much heartier puff panini would be just as good for when the guys come over for the big game as it is for a cocktail party.

1. Preheat the oven to 350°F. In a bowl combine ground beef, egg, bread crumbs, onion, milk, ketchup, cheese, salt, and pepper. Mash all the ingredients together with your hands until well mixed, and then form into ball shapes. The meatballs should be on the small side, about the size of a golf ball or smaller.

2. Place on a broiler pan and bake for 20–30 minutes.

3. Preheat the panini press. Place the pastry sheets on panini press and leave the lid open. Cook for 2–3 minutes, then remove from press and set aside.

4. Slice meatballs in half or quarters and place on the cooked side of 4 pastry sheets. Place the remaining four sheets on top, with the cooked side facing inward. Place on panini press and cook for an additional 2–3 minutes.

5. Remove from press and place on a cutting board. Use a pizza cutter to cut each panini into four bite-sized pieces. Serve warm.

INGREDIENTS | SERVES 2

4 (5" square) puff pastry sheets
1 portobello mushroom cap
2 tablespoons olive oil
2 tablespoons butter
1 chopped shallot
1 teaspoon thyme
1 teaspoon parsley
2 tablespoons dry white wine
4 tablespoons grated Parmesan cheese

Portobello Parmesan Puff Panini

This mushroom appetizer is easy to make in advance. Just spread the filling onto puff pastry at party time.

1. Preheat the panini press. Place the pastry sheets on panini press and leave the lid open. Cook for 2–3 minutes, then remove from press and set aside.

2. Place portobello on the panini press and drizzle with olive oil. Close lid and cook for 4–6 minutes. Chop the mushroom and set aside.

3. Place butter in a frying pan and add shallot, thyme, parsley, and wine and sauté for 1–2 minutes. Add chopped mushroom to the pan and cook for 1–2 minutes. Spoon mushroom mixture onto cooked side of 2 pastry sheets, then add grated Parmesan cheese on top. Close sandwiches with remaining pastry sheets with the cooked side facing inside. Return to panini press, close lid, and cook for an additional 1–2 minutes.

4. Remove from press and place on a cutting board. Use a pizza cutter to cut each panini into four bite-sized pieces. Serve warm.

Dijon Crab Puff Panini

INGREDIENTS | SERVES 4

6 (5" square) puff pastry sheets
¼ cup lump crabmeat
¼ cup mayonnaise
5 tablespoons cream cheese
¼ cup chives
2 tablespoons Dijon mustard
2 tablespoons lemon juice

Puff pastry sheets come in a few different sizes. Five-inch squares are best for cocktail party appetizers.

1. Preheat the panini press. Place the pastry sheets on panini press and leave the lid open. Cook for 2–3 minutes, remove from press, and set aside.

2. Mix the rest of the ingredients in a bowl and spread the mixture onto the cooked sides of 3 pastry sheets. Close sandwiches with remaining pastry sheets with the cooked sides facing in. Return to panini press, close lid, and cook for an additional 1–2 minutes.

3. Remove from press and place on a cutting board. Use a pizza cutter to cut each panini into four bite-sized pieces. Serve warm.

Cuban Quesadilla

INGREDIENTS | SERVES 2

2 flour tortillas
2 slices ham
2 slices roast pork
1 sliced pickle
2 slices Swiss cheese
1 tablespoon mustard

This quesadilla makes a great appetizer. Cut it with a pizza cutter before serving it to your guests.

1. Preheat the panini press. Place the flour tortillas on a cutting board. Lay ham, pork, pickle slices, and Swiss cheese on half of each tortilla. Spread mustard on the other half of each tortilla, and then fold the tortilla in half so that it's shaped like a half circle.

2. Place on panini press and close lid.

3. Cook for 3–5 minutes.

4. Remove from press and place on a cutting board. Use a pizza cutter to cut each panini into four triangle-shaped pieces. Serve warm.

2 slices bacon

4 ripe figs

2 slices Italian panella bread, sliced ¼" thick

2 tablespoons goat cheese

1 teaspoon balsamic vinegar

2 teaspoons honey

Figs with Goat Cheese and Bacon Panini

You may have had bacon-wrapped figs at a cocktail party as an hors d'oeuvre. You can make a lot of appetizers panini style, just like in this recipe.

1. Preheat the panini press. Cook bacon on panini press until crisp and set aside.

2. Cut figs in half lengthwise and place skin side up on panini press. Leave the lid open and cook for 3–5 minutes. Remove from press. Cut figs into slices and lay them onto 1 slice of bread. Add the goat cheese and then drizzle with balsamic vinegar and honey. Top with bacon and close sandwich with remaining slice of bread.

3. Place sandwich on the panini press, close lid, and cook for 2–3 minutes or until bread is crispy.

4. Remove from press and slice in half. Serve warm.

Black Mission Figs

Black Mission figs are very sweet figs, and if they're very fresh, they'll even ooze a syrupy juice when you cut them. They are close to black or purple in color and have a pink flesh.

4 figs
2 slices Italian bread
2 tablespoons mascarpone cheese
1 tablespoon butter
1 teaspoon brown sugar

Grilled Figs with Mascarpone Panini

If you're lucky enough to know someone who has a fig tree, you should offer them some panini sandwiches in exchange for fresh figs. This caramelized fig panini with mascarpone cheese is worth about a bushel of fresh figs.

1. Preheat the panini press. Cut figs in half lengthwise and place skin side up on panini press. Leave the lid open and cook for 3–5 minutes. Remove from press. Cut figs into slices and lay them on 1 slice of bread. Add the mascarpone cheese. On the other slice of bread spread the butter, and then sprinkle it with brown sugar.

2. Put the two halves of the sandwich together and place it on the panini press. Close the lid and cook for 2–3 minutes or until bread is crispy.

3. Remove from press and slice in half. Serve warm.

Variations

If you can't find mascarpone cheese, ricotta can be used as a substitute.

CHAPTER 14

Panini for Kids

INGREDIENTS | SERVES 1

1 hot dog
2 slices white bread
1 slice American cheese
2 tablespoons ketchup

Hot Dog Panini

Even if you don't have a hot dog bun, you can still make a hot dog panini for your favorite kid with regular bread. The panini grill makes it nice and crispy.

1. Preheat the panini press. Place hot dog on panini press and close lid. Cook for 3–5 minutes, then place the cooked hot dog on a cutting board. Cut the hot dog into 1" sections. Arrange hot dog sections on 1 slice of bread.

2. Add the cheese, and then spread the ketchup on a second slice of bread and cover.

3. Cook for 2–3 minutes.

4. Remove from press, cut in half, and serve with additional ketchup for dipping.

Variations

What ever toppings the children usually eat on a regular hot dog can be added to a hot dog panini as well. Try relish, mustard, sauerkraut, or even chili.

1 hot pretzel
2 slices Cheddar cheese
1 tablespoon mustard

Hot Pretzel and Cheese Panini

A sliced hot pretzel can make a tasty substitution for the bread in a panini. Add some cheese and you've got two favorites in one. You'll want a fresh pretzel that's still soft for this panini.

1. Carefully slice pretzel in half sandwich style.

2. Add cheese slices on top of one side. You may want to cut cheese into strips and only lay it on the pretzel. Any cheese without pretzel underneath it will melt onto the panini press.

3. Spread mustard on second half of pretzel. Replace top of pretzel and line up sides with bottom.

4. Place on panini press, close lid, and cook for 2–3 minutes.

5. Remove from press and serve warm.

INGREDIENTS | SERVES 1

1 flour tortilla
2 tablespoons tomato sauce
½ cup shredded mozzarella cheese

Pizza Panini

Pizza is another popular kids' meal that can be made panini style. You can even use a pizza cutter to cut it into triangles.

1. Preheat the panini press. Place the tortilla on a cutting board. Spread tomato sauce on half of the tortilla. Then add cheese and fold the tortilla in half.

2. Place on panini press and close lid.

3. Cook for 3–5 minutes.

4. Remove from press and place on a cutting board.

5. Using a pizza cutter, cut the panini into four triangles. Serve warm.

Pizza Panini Variations

You can add whatever your child will eat on a regular pizza onto a pizza panini. Popular toppings include pepperoni, sausage, and mushrooms. You could also sneak a few vegetables in there. The familiar taste of the tomato sauce and mozzarella cheese will make them think they're eating pizza, and they might not notice the small amount of broccoli that is stowing away in there. Chop the broccoli first and fry it in garlic and oil to make it taste more like it belongs on a pizza.

Spaghetti and Meatball Panini

You'll need some leftover spaghetti and meatballs for this panini. And you'll need a good quality Italian-style loaf of bread that you can cut into ¼" slices. Next time you make pasta for dinner, put aside a few servings with sauce into the fridge. Then it'll be a snap to make this fun panini for your kids whenever they're hungry.

1. In a large bowl add spaghetti and meatballs. If meatballs are large, you may want to slice or chop them first. Add mozzarella cheese and mix.

2. Preheat the panini press. Scoop spaghetti mixture onto 2 slices of bread. Do not overfill. If you use more than a ½" layer of spaghetti, the panini will fall apart.

3. Close sandwiches with 2 more slices of bread and place on panini press. Close the lid and cook for 3–5 minutes.

4. Remove from press and cut in half. Serve with tomato sauce for dunking.

Spaghetti Tacos

Spaghetti tacos seem to be the rage among the tween crowd lately due in part to a popular TV show. You can make this recipe with soft corn tortillas if you want to see what all the buzz is about.

Ham and Cheese Panini

Sometimes a simple panini is the way to go when cooking for children. You can add extra ingredients, like a few tomato slices, or jazz it up with different cheeses if you are feeding a good eater. But keep the panini simple if he or she is finicky.

1. Preheat the panini press. On 1 slice of bread add the ham slices and cheese.

2. Top panini with second slice of bread and place on panini press. Close the lid and cook for 3–5 minutes.

3. Remove from press, cut in half, and serve warm.

Chicken Nugget and Mozzarella Sticks Panini

This panini may scare away the grownups, but that's okay because it's designed for kids. Sorry, there's no toy included in this meal!

1. Cook the chicken nuggets and mozzarella sticks according to instructions on the packages.

2. Preheat the panini press. Cut open a roll. Add the chicken nuggets, mozzarella sticks, and a few spoonfuls of tomato sauce.

3. Place on panini press, close lid, and cook for 3–5 minutes.

4. Remove from press, cut in half, and serve warm with tomato sauce for dunking.

1 tablespoon butter

2 slices white or wheat bread

2 tablespoons peanut butter

2 tablespoons jelly

Peanut Butter and Jelly Panini

Peanut butter and jelly is even better when it's made in a panini press.

1. Preheat the panini press. Spread butter onto one side of each slice of bread. Then spread the peanut butter on the nonbuttered side of 1 slice of bread.

2. Spread jelly onto the nonbuttered side of the other slice of bread.

3. Put slices together. Place on panini press and close the lid.

4. Cook for 3–4 minutes.

5. Remove from press, cut in half, and serve warm.

Powdered Sugar

A dusting of powdered sugar adds a sweet touch to any panini. Just tell your kids it's snow.

INGREDIENTS | **SERVES 1**

2 strips bacon
½ cup leftover macaroni and cheese
2 slices white or wheat bread

Mac and Cheese Panini

This panini may sound a little odd, but kids really love it.

1. Preheat the panini press. Place bacon strips on panini press and cook until crisp. Remove and set aside to cool.

2. In a bowl add the macaroni and cheese. Crumble the bacon and sprinkle over the top of the macaroni and cheese, then give it a good mix to distribute the bacon evenly. Spoon the macaroni and cheese mixture onto 1 slice of bread to create a thin (¼"–½") layer. Leave some room at the edges of bread so that the panini seals shut.

3. Place on panini press and close the lid. Cook for 3–5 minutes.

4. Remove from press, cut in half, and serve warm.

Variations

You can replace the bacon with ham and add a tablespoon of salsa to make it a little spicier.

Peanut Butter and Banana Panini

Honey and cinnamon can make almost anything taste excellent. Peanut butter and banana are no exception. Stick with a sweet or soft bread for this recipe.

1. Preheat the panini press. On 1 slice of bread spread the peanut butter. Drizzle it with honey and sprinkle on cinnamon. Add the banana slices and top with the second slice of bread.

2. Place on panini press, close lid, and cook for 2–4 minutes.

3. Remove from press, cut in half, and serve warm.

Marshmallow Cream and Peanut Butter Panini

Who didn't enjoy a fluffer nutter sandwich as a kid? Introduce your kids to this classic treat.

1. Preheat the panini press. On 1 slice of bread spread the peanut butter. On the other slice of bread spread the marshmallow cream. Close the sandwich.

2. Place on panini press and cook for 2–4 minutes.

3. Remove from press, cut in half, and serve warm.

INGREDIENTS | SERVES 1

1 Snickers bar
2 slices white or wheat bread

Snickers Sandwich

You'll be surprised at how good this tastes. You'll want to use a sweet bread or even angel food cake for this panini. Don't be afraid to experiment with all of your favorite candy bars.

1. Preheat the panini press. Cut a Snickers bar into small slices and add them to 1 slice of bread. Top the sandwich with another slice of bread and place on panini press.

2. Close lid and cook for 2–4 minutes, then remove from press.

3. Cut in half and serve warm.

CHAPTER 15

Leftover Sandwiches

2 slices Italian bread or 1 Kaiser roll
2 thick slices turkey
¼ cup stuffing
4 tablespoons gravy

Thanksgiving Leftover Panini

You may have enjoyed leftover turkey sandwiches in the past, but you can use up even more Thanksgiving leftovers with this panini. Too bad Thanksgiving only comes once a year.

1. Preheat the panini press. On your work surface, place 1 slice of bread or the bottom half of the roll. Add turkey and stuffing. Pour gravy on top of ingredients and on the other slice of bread or the other half of the roll.

2. Close sandwich and place on panini press.

3. Close lid and cook for 3–5 minutes.

4. Remove from press, slice in half, and serve with a small cup of hot gravy for dipping.

INGREDIENTS | SERVES 1

1 or 2 slices meatloaf (½" thick)
2 slices Italian bread or Kaiser roll
2 slices Cheddar cheese
2 tablespoons ketchup

Leftover Meatloaf Panini

When you fill a baking pan with meatloaf, there's bound to be leftovers. Your panini press is the perfect way to reheat and enhance your leftover meatloaf. No more microwave sandwiches for you!

1. Preheat the panini press. Add meatloaf to 1 slice of bread or bottom half of roll. Place Cheddar cheese on top of meatloaf. Pour ketchup on top and close sandwich. You may want to add ketchup to both sides of bread if meatloaf is on the dry side.

2. Place on panini press and close lid.

3. Cook for 3–5 minutes.

4. Remove from press and cut in half. Serve warm.

Leftover chicken marsala
2 slices Italian bread or a Kaiser roll

Leftover Chicken Marsala Panini

After a catered party, you may find that you have an extra tray or two of chicken marsala. The best way to use up those leftovers is between crusty bread. And the best way to reheat it is with your panini press.

1. Preheat panini press.

2. Add leftover chicken marsala to 1 slice of bread or bottom half of roll. Be sure to scoop up any juices and pour them onto the bread.

3. Close sandwich and place on panini press.

4. Close lid and cook for 3–5 minutes, then remove from press.

5. Cut in half and serve warm.

Leftover Glazed Ham with Brie on French Bread

INGREDIENTS | SERVES 1

2–4 slices leftover glazed ham
3 slices Brie cheese
2 slices French bread
Dijon mustard, to taste

Cooking a glazed ham for the holidays is always a popular choice. They come precooked and all you have to do is reheat and glaze it. And, of course, there's always leftover ham that you can make this panini recipe with.

1. Preheat the panini press. Lay ham and Brie on 1 slice of bread. Spread Dijon mustard on other slice of bread and close sandwich. Place on panini press and close lid.

2. Cook for 3–5 minutes.

3. Remove from press and serve warm.

Meatball Parmesan Panini

INGREDIENTS | SERVES 1

1 Portuguese or Kaiser roll
3–5 meatballs
3 slices mozzarella cheese
2 tablespoons tomato sauce

This popular hero can be made panini style with the help of some leftover meatballs and some mozzarella cheese.

1. Cut roll in half and add meatballs to bottom half of sandwich. You may want to cut the meatballs in half, depending on how big they are.

2. Add the mozzarella cheese and tomato sauce, then replace the top of the roll.

3. Place on panini press, close lid, and cook for 3–5 minutes.

4. Remove from panini press, cut in half, and serve with a small bowl of tomato sauce for dunking.

4–6 ounces leftover eggplant Parmesan

2 slices Italian bread or a Portuguese roll

¼ cup tomato sauce

Leftover Eggplant Parmesan Panini

Eggplant Parmesan is a popular holiday meal in Italian families. It's usually made in a large tray, so it's common to have leftovers no matter how many family members you have. You'll want to use crunchy Italian bread for this one.

1. Preheat the panini press. Place leftover eggplant Parmesan on 1 slice of bread or bottom half of roll and pour tomato sauce on top of eggplant.

2. Top with another slice of bread and place on panini press.

3. Close lid and cook for 3–5 minutes; remove from press.

4. Cut in half and serve with a small bowl of hot tomato sauce for dipping.

4–6 ounces leftover pulled pork
1 ciabatta roll
2 slices Cheddar cheese

Leftover Pulled Pork Panini

Tender pork, cooked for hours and slathered with barbecue sauce, is too good to waste. Grab a ciabatta roll and get busy.

1. Preheat the panini press. Cut roll in half, and scoop or use tongs to put the leftover pulled pork onto the roll.

2. Add Cheddar cheese slices on top of pork.

3. Replace top of roll and place on panini press.

4. Close lid and cook for 3–5 minutes; remove from panini press.

5. Don't bother cutting this panini in half—serve with extra napkins.

2 tablespoons olive oil

1 small onion, sliced

1 small bell pepper, sliced

1 teaspoon garlic powder

Salt and pepper, to taste

2 eggs

4–6 ounces leftover steak

1 Portuguese or Kaiser roll

1 teaspoon Worcestershire sauce

Steak and Egg Panini

Steak and eggs are a treat that you probably don't often make for yourself. Why cook an entire steak for a panini when you can just use leftovers instead?

1. Preheat the panini press. Pour olive oil into a bowl and add onion and pepper. Sprinkle with garlic powder, salt, and pepper. Mix until evenly coated, and empty bowl on panini press. Cook for 3–5 minutes. Remove from press and set aside.

2. In a pan coated with nonstick cooking spray, fry or scramble two eggs and set aside.

3. Slice leftover steak and place on bottom half of roll. Add eggs and grilled onion and pepper. Then top with Worcestershire sauce.

4. Close sandwich. Place on panini press, close lid, and cook for 2–3 minutes.

5. Remove from panini press and cut in half. Serve warm.

2 tablespoons minced garlic

3 tablespoons olive oil

½ cup chopped crimini mushrooms

1 Portuguese or Kaiser roll

¼ pound sliced cooked filet mignon

2 tablespoons Garlic Mayonnaise (see Chapter 19)

Filet Mignon and Garlic Mushroom Panini

Crimini mushrooms are baby portobello mushrooms and are sometimes sold as Baby Bellas. Button mushrooms will also do in a pinch.

1. Preheat the panini press. In a bowl combine the garlic, olive oil, and crimini mushrooms. Pour the contents onto panini press and cook for 2–4 minutes. Remove from press and set aside.

2. Cut open the roll and arrange the filet mignon slices. Place the mushrooms on top. Spread the Garlic Mayonnaise on the top half of the roll and close sandwich.

3. Place on panini press and close the lid.

4. Cook for 3–5 minutes. Remove from press and slice in half. Serve warm.

1 cup chopped leftover frittata

2 slices Italian bread

¼ cup Cheddar cheese

Leftover Frittata Panini

A frittata or a quiche is a great dish to serve at a brunch gathering. But what do you do with the leftovers? If you have a panini press, you already know the answer to that question.

1. Preheat the panini press. Scoop a portion of frittata onto 1 slice of bread. If it's a thick frittata, you may want to chop it up a little to make a panini that fits in your mouth.

2. Add cheese and top sandwich with the other slice of bread.

3. Place on panini press and close lid.

4. Cook for 3–5 minutes.

5. Remove from press, cut in half, and serve warm.

Grilled Chicken, Black Beans, and Cheddar Panini

Lots of people fire up the barbecue on the weekends and grill meats to be used in meals during the week. If you have leftover chicken breast, this is a great way to use it up Mexican style.

1. Preheat the panini press. Slice chicken breast into bite-sized pieces. In a bowl mix sliced chicken breast, black beans, and Salsa.

2. Slice the roll in half. Empty contents of the bowl onto the bottom half of the roll. Add Cheddar cheese and replace top on roll. Put on panini press and close the lid.

3. Cook for 3–5 minutes.

4. Remove from panini press and cut in half.

5. Serve with extra Salsa and sour cream.

INGREDIENTS | SERVES 1

1 small onion, sliced
1 Portuguese or Kaiser roll
4–6 ounces leftover roast beef
2 slices pepper jack cheese
2 tablespoons ranch dressing

Leftover Roast Beef Panini

Roast beef is as delicious leftover as it is the first day. If you don't have a meat slicer, be sure to cut your roast beef into thin slices for this panini.

1. Preheat the panini press. Grill onions on panini press for 2–4 minutes and set aside.

2. Slice roll in half. Place leftover roast beef on bottom half of roll. Add pepper jack cheese and grilled onions. Then pour ranch dressing on top of cheese and onions.

3. Cap with top of roll and place on panini press.

4. Close lid and cook for 3–5 minutes.

5. Remove from press, slice in half, and serve warm.

INGREDIENTS | SERVES 1

2 cooked pork chops
2 slices honey oat bread
½ apple, peeled and thinly sliced
4 slices Gouda cheese

Pork Chops, Apple, and Gouda Panini

Boneless pork cutlets, pork chops, or even roast pork loin can be used to make this panini.

1. Preheat the panini press. Chop pork into bite-sized pieces.

2. Arrange pork pieces on 1 slice of bread.

3. Place the apple slices on the pork, and then lay the Gouda cheese on top. Close the sandwich and place on panini press.

4. Close lid and cook for 3–4 minutes, then remove from press.

5. Cut in half and serve warm.

Variation
Add some butter and cinnamon to the apples to make a sweeter panini.

CHAPTER 16

Pressed Desserts

5 tablespoons creamy peanut butter
2 slices bread
1 banana, peeled and sliced
2 tablespoons Nutella
Powdered sugar, to taste

Peanut Butter, Banana, and Nutella Panini

Since this panini makes for a great dessert or snack, you'll want to use a soft, sweet bread. Try a nice honey wheat loaf from the supermarket or challah bread from the bakery.

1. Preheat the panini press. Spread the peanut butter onto 1 slice of bread.

2. Place banana slices on the peanut butter-coated slice of bread.

3. Spread the Nutella on the other slice of bread and put the two slices of bread together.

4. Place on panini press and close. Cook for 2–5 minutes.

5. Remove from press and slice in half. Serve with a dusting of powdered sugar.

Nutella

Nutella is a popular chocolate hazelnut spread, and it really adds a nice flavor to this panini. Milk chocolate, semisweet chocolate, or dark chocolate chips can also be used if you are unable to find Nutella in the store. Another option would be to use a premium chocolate bar and grate it with a microplane.

Pound Cake with Strawberries and Nutella

You don't have to use bread to make a panini. Let them eat cake.

1. Preheat the panini press. Spread 1 slice of pound cake with Nutella.

2. Add strawberries on top of Nutella. Top panini with second slice of pound cake.

3. Place on panini press, close lid, and cook for 2–4 minutes.

4. Remove from press and cut in half. Serve warm with whipped cream or a sprinkle of powdered sugar.

Gingerbread, Cream Cheese, and Raspberry Jam Panini

Whether it's jelly, jam, fruit butter, or chutney, it's all welcome here in this dessert panini. If you don't have jam, use what you have on hand.

1. Preheat the panini press. Spread cream cheese on 1 slice of gingerbread, and spread the raspberry jam on the other slice.

2. Put the two halves together and place on panini press. Close lid and cook for 2–4 minutes.

3. Remove from press and cut in half. Serve warm with a sprinkle of powdered sugar.

Ice Cream Panini

If serving these at a party, make the puff pastry sheets in advance and keep them warm. Then scoop out the ice cream when you're ready to serve.

1. Preheat the panini press. Place the puff pastry on panini press and close the lid. Cook for 2–4 minutes and remove.

2. Spoon ice cream onto one puff pastry sheet and top with the other to make an ice cream sandwich. Be careful not to crack the pastry sheets.

3. Serve immediately.

INGREDIENTS | SERVES 1

3 tablespoons marshmallow cream
2 slices challah bread
3 tablespoons chocolate chips
4 crushed graham crackers

S'mores Panini

Why wait for your next camping trip to make s'mores when you can make them in your panini press? Use a sweet bread to hold it together, and crush some graham crackers to add to the panini filling.

1. Preheat the panini press. Spread the marshmallow cream on 1 slice of bread, and top with chocolate chips and crushed graham crackers. Top with the other slice of challah bread.

2. Place on panini press, close lid, and cook for 2–4 minutes.

3. Remove from press and cut in half. Serve warm.

2 slices pound cake (¼" to ½" thick)

4 tablespoons mascarpone cheese

¼ cup fresh blueberries

Pound Cake with Mascarpone Cheese and Berries

Mascarpone cheese is milky and creamy. It spreads really well and is sometimes used to make tiramisu.

1. Preheat the panini press. Spread 1 slice of pound cake with mascarpone cheese.

2. Add the blueberries and top panini with second slice of pound cake.

3. Place on panini press, close lid, and cook for 2–4 minutes.

4. Remove from press and cut in half. Serve warm with whipped cream or a sprinkle of powdered sugar.

Frozen Berry Mixes

This recipe works great with frozen berry medleys, which usually include blueberries, raspberries, strawberries, and blackberries. These frozen mixes are perfect for the dead of winter when you don't have fresh fruit in the house. Let them thaw before adding them to the panini.

INGREDIENTS | SERVES 1

3 tablespoons raspberry jam
2 slices cinnamon bread
3 tablespoons ricotta cheese
3 tablespoons chocolate chips

Cinnamon, Chocolate, and Raspberry Panini

Ricotta cheese is similar in texture to cottage cheese but is much lighter. It's an Italian cheese that can be made from sheep's milk, and it's usually served with pasta.

1. Preheat the panini press. Spread the raspberry jam on 1 slice of cinnamon bread and the ricotta cheese on the other. Sprinkle the chocolate chips on the jam side, and close the sandwich together.

2. Place on panini press, close lid, and cook for 2–4 minutes.

3. Remove from press and cut in half. Serve warm with whipped cream or a sprinkle of powdered sugar.

Ricotta Cheese

Ricotta cheese isn't just for lasagna or baked ziti. It's used in a lot of Italian desserts such as cheesecake, tiramisu, and, of course, in paninis.

1 apple, peeled, cored, and sliced
2 tablespoons butter
½ teaspoon cinnamon
2 teaspoons brown sugar
Pinch nutmeg, to taste
2 puff pastry sheets

Apple Pie Panini Pastry

Puff pastry sheets are just like flaky pie crusts when heated in a panini press. Be sure to try all of your favorite pie fillings in a panini.

1. Place apple slices in a small frying pan over medium heat. Add butter, cinnamon, and sugar and cook for about 4 minutes while stirring constantly. Add a pinch of nutmeg if desired. While the apple slices are cooking, preheat the panini press.

2. Place the puff pastry on panini press and do not close the lid. Cook for 2–4 minutes and remove. Scoop a portion of the apple mixture onto the center of one cooked side of the puff pastry sheet, leaving room at the edges for a good seal. Add the other puff pastry sheet to form a sandwich, with the uncooked sides facing outward. Don't overstuff your pastry puff sheets.

3. Close lid and cook for 3–5 minutes.

4. Remove from press and cut in half. Serve warm with a scoop of ice cream or a sprinkle of powdered sugar.

Time Saver

There are many different types of pie fillings that are available in a can. Cans of cherry, strawberry, and even sweet potato pie fillings may be waiting for you at your local supermarket. Just scoop and press.

1 large square coffee cake
3 tablespoons strawberry jam

Inside Out Coffee Cake Panini

You can turn everyday coffee cake into a warm, fruit-filled dessert.

1. Preheat the panini press. Cut the piece of coffee cake in half lengthwise. Spread jam onto the bottom slice of coffee cake. Replace the top slice of cake, but turn it upside down so that the crumbs are facing inside the panini.

2. Place on panini press, close lid, and cook for 2–4 minutes.

3. Remove from press and cut in half. Serve warm.

Variations

Use your favorite jam, jelly, or even fresh fruit to fill this panini. Or leave out the fruit and fill it with chocolate chips and a sprinkle of cinnamon.

Blueberry Angel Food Panini

Angel food cake is a light and airy cake. Using it in a panini sandwich is heavenly.

INGREDIENTS | SERVES 1

2 slices angel food cake (¼" to ½" thick)
3 tablespoons blueberry jam
Powdered sugar, to taste

1. Preheat the panini press. Spread 1 slice of cake with jam, and top with the other slice of cake.

2. Place on panini press, close lid, and cook for 2–4 minutes.

3. Remove from press and cut in half. Serve warm with a dusting of powdered sugar.

Pineapple and Cream Cheese Panini

You can use whipped cream cheese or ricotta if you like a lighter, fluffier panini. Try a honey oat bread or another sweet bread with this one.

INGREDIENTS | SERVES 1

2 slices bread
3 tablespoons cream cheese
4 slices pineapple

1. Preheat the panini press. On 1 slice of bread spread the cream cheese and add the pineapple slices. Top sandwich with the other slice of bread.

2. Place on panini press, close lid, and cook for 3–5 minutes.

3. Remove from press, cut in half, and serve warm.

Peanut Butter, Chocolate, and Marshmallow Cream Panini

Marshmallow cream is an underutilized ingredient in today's sandwiches. This panini is a step toward fixing that.

1. Preheat the panini press. On 1 slice of bread spread the peanut butter and sprinkle with chocolate chips. On the other slice of bread spread the marshmallow cream. Put the two halves of the sandwich together.

2. Place on panini press, close lid, and cook for 2–4 minutes.

3. Remove from press and cut in half. Serve warm with a dusting of powdered sugar.

Bread Choices

You would think that sweet bread would be required for this panini, but really any bread can be quick and tasty when paired with peanut butter, chocolate, and marshmallow cream. Just stay clear of rye or pumpernickel.

Panini Wontons

INGREDIENTS | **SERVES 2**

4 ounces cream cheese

6 ounces lump crabmeat

2 scallions, thinly sliced

12 wonton wrappers

Crab Wontons

Wonton wrappers are sold in most specialty supermarkets.

1. Mix cream cheese, crab, and scallions in a bowl with a wooden spoon until well blended.

2. On a wonton wrapper, add a spoonful of the filling and wet the edges with your finger or a basting brush. Lay another wonton wrapper on top and seal the edges well, using more water as necessary. Set aside. Repeat the wonton-filling process until you are out of the filling or wontons. Preheat the panini press.

3. Place wontons on panini press and gently close the lid. Cook for 3–5 minutes or until wontons are crisp.

4. Remove from press and serve warm.

Substitutions

If you can't find wonton wrappers at the store, try egg roll skins or spring roll pasta sheets. Broiled shrimp that's been chopped can replace the lump crabmeat.

½ pound ground pork
8 ounces water chestnuts
4 scallions
½ teaspoon minced ginger
2 teaspoons sesame oil
2 teaspoons soy sauce
1 tablespoon rice wine
½ teaspoon cornstarch
½ teaspoon salt
Pinch white pepper
20 wonton wrappers

Pork Wontons

You'll be tempted to overfill these wontons because the filling is very tasty. However, to make wontons on a panini press, they must stay thin.

1. In a frying pan brown the ground pork for 3–5 minutes. Remove from pan and drain the fat, then set aside. Chop the water chestnuts and scallions, and add to a bowl with the ginger. In another bowl combine the sesame oil, soy sauce, rice wine, and cornstarch and mix until cornstarch is dissolved. Pour cornstarch mixture over the water chestnuts and scallions, and then add the pork. Add the salt and white pepper and then stir until well mixed.

2. On a wonton wrapper, add a spoonful of the filling and wet the edges with your finger or a basting brush. Lay another wonton wrapper on top and seal the edges well, using more water if necessary. Set aside. Repeat the wonton-filling process until you are out of the filling or wontons. Preheat the panini press.

3. Place wontons on panini press and gently close the lid. Cook for 3–5 minutes or until wontons are crisp.

4. Remove from press and serve warm.

INGREDIENTS | SERVES 2

16 wonton wrappers
6 ounces Nutella

Nutella Wontons

Wontons for dessert? Why not?

1. On a wonton wrapper, add a spoonful of Nutella and wet the edges with your finger or a basting brush. Lay another wonton wrapper on top and seal the edges well, using more water if necessary. Set aside. Repeat the wonton-filling process until you are out of the filling or wontons. Preheat the panini press.

2. Place wontons on the panini press and gently close the lid. Cook for 3–5 minutes or until wontons are crisp.

3. Remove from press and serve warm.

Variation

Add a pinch of cinnamon to these wontons before you close them up. With all wonton panini recipes, you can make them square shaped using two wonton wrappers or triangle shaped using just one.

Chicken Wontons

Panini wontons have distinctive grill marks. Tell those wimpy steamed wontons to go home.

1. In a frying pan brown the ground chicken for 3–5 minutes. Remove from pan and drain the fat, then set aside. Place shallot and scallions in a bowl. Add the garlic, soy sauce, ginger, sesame oil, lime juice, sugar, and chicken. Stir until well mixed.

2. On a wonton wrapper, add a spoonful of the filling and wet the edges with your finger or a basting brush. Lay another wonton wrapper on top and seal the edges well, using more water if necessary. Set aside. Repeat the wonton-filling process until you are out of the filling or wontons. Preheat the panini press.

3. Place wontons on panini press and gently close the lid. Cook for 3–5 minutes or until the wontons are crisp.

4. Remove from press and serve warm.

INGREDIENTS | SERVES 2

10 wonton wrappers
1 banana, peeled and sliced
½ cup chocolate chips
1 tablespoon cinnamon

Banana Wontons

It will only take you a few minutes to make these dessert wontons. It will be time well spent!

1. On a wonton wrapper, add a banana slice, a few chocolate chips, and a sprinkle of cinnamon. Then wet the edges of the wonton with your finger or a basting brush. Lay another wonton wrapper on top and seal the edges well, using more water if necessary. Set aside. Repeat the wonton-filling process until you are out of the filling or wontons. Preheat the panini press.

2. Place wontons on the panini press and gently close the lid. Cook for 3–5 minutes or until wontons are crisp.

3. Remove from press and serve warm with a dollop of whipped cream.

INGREDIENTS | SERVES 4

½ pound ground pork

2 teaspoons sesame oil

1 teaspoon lime juice

1 teaspoon sugar

⅔ cup chopped bok choy

3 chopped scallions

3 chopped shiitake mushrooms

1 tablespoon minced garlic

2 teaspoons soy sauce

½ teaspoon grated ginger

20 wonton wrappers

Pork and Mushroom Wontons

Wontons will make good appetizers at your next party. You can make them in your panini press beforehand and place them on cookie sheets for reheating in the oven when it's party time.

1. In a frying pan brown the ground pork for 3–5 minutes. Remove from pan and drain the fat, then set aside. In a preheated frying pan add the sesame oil, lime juice, and sugar and stir. Add the bok choy, scallions, mushrooms, garlic, soy sauce, and ginger and fry for 3–5 minutes. Remove from heat and let cool for about 5 minutes, then add to ground pork.

2. On a wonton wrapper, add a spoonful of the filling and wet the edges with your finger or a basting brush. Lay another wonton wrapper on top and seal the edges well, using more water if necessary. Set aside. Repeat the wonton-filling process until you are out of the filling or wontons. Preheat the panini press.

3. Place wontons on panini press and gently close the lid. Cook for 3–5 minutes or until wontons are crisp.

4. Remove from press and serve warm.

Variations
Napa cabbage can replace the bok choy in this recipe.

15 medium shrimp, peeled and deveined

8 ounces water chestnuts, chopped

4 scallions, thinly sliced

½ teaspoon ground ginger

1 tablespoon oyster sauce

2 teaspoons sesame oil

2 teaspoons soy sauce

1 tablespoon rice wine

½ teaspoon cornstarch

½ teaspoon salt

Pinch white pepper

20 wonton wrappers

Shrimp Wontons

You can skip the wonton wrappers and make these with egg roll skins. Just keep them thin and long so that they heat evenly.

1. Preheat the panini press. Peel shrimp, then place on panini press. Close lid and cook for 2–4 minutes; set aside. Place water chestnuts and scallions in a bowl with the ginger. In another bowl combine the oyster sauce, sesame oil, soy sauce, rice wine, and the cornstarch and mix until cornstarch is dissolved. Pour cornstarch mixture over the water chestnuts and scallions. Chop the shrimp and then add it to the bowl. Add the salt and white pepper and then stir until well mixed.

2. On a wonton wrapper, add a spoonful of the filling and wet the edges with your finger or a basting brush. Lay another wonton wrapper on top and seal the edges well, using more water if necessary. Set aside. Repeat the wonton-filling process until you are out of the filling or wontons. Preheat the panini press.

3. Place wontons on panini press and gently close the lid. Cook for 3–5 minutes or until wontons are crisp.

4. Remove from press and serve warm.

2 baked Yukon Gold potatoes
½ cup Colby cheese
2 scallions, chopped
2 tablespoons sour cream
20 wonton wrappers

Potato Cheese Wontons

This wonton may remind you of a stuffed baked potato or a pierogie.

1. Peel the skins off baked potatoes and discard. Place the potatoes in a food processor with the cheese, scallions, and sour cream. Process until well blended.

2. On a wonton wrapper, add a spoonful of the filling and wet the edges with your finger or a basting brush. Lay another wonton wrapper on top and seal the edges well, using more water if necessary. Set aside. Repeat the wonton-filling process until you are out of the filling or wontons. Preheat the panini press.

3. Place wontons on panini press and gently close the lid. Cook for 3–5 minutes or until wontons are crisp.

4. Remove from press and serve warm.

Variations

The addition of crumbled bacon or chopped sausage will satisfy the meat lovers at your dinner table. Or try chopped broccoli that is sautéed in garlic and oil for vegetarians.

Apple Cinnamon Wontons

These crispy, bite-sized apple pies will be a hit at your next party.

1. Place apple in a small frying pan over medium heat. Add butter, sugar, cinnamon, and nutmeg, then cook for about 4 minutes while stirring constantly. Remove from heat and let cool for a few minutes.

2. On a wonton wrapper, add a spoonful of the filling and wet the edges with your finger or a basting brush. Lay another wonton wrapper on top and seal the edges well, using more water if necessary. Set aside. Repeat the wonton-filling process until you are out of the filling or wontons. Preheat the panini press.

3. Place wontons on panini press and gently close the lid. Cook for 3–5 minutes or until wontons are crisp.

4. Remove from press and serve warm.

INGREDIENTS | SERVES 4

½ pound ground beef

1 packet taco seasoning

¼ cup chopped onion

1 tablespoon jalapeño pepper slices

¼ cup Cheddar cheese

Taco Wontons

Want to serve tacos at your next party but afraid of the mess? Why not seal up those tacos in wonton wrappers? They make a nice, neat appetizer.

1. In a frying pan brown the ground beef. Remove from pan and drain the fat, then set aside. Add the taco seasoning and water, if directions on packet call for it.

2. Add onion, jalapeño pepper, and Cheddar cheese and mix well.

3. On a wonton wrapper, add a spoonful of the filling and wet the edges with your finger or a basting brush. Lay another wonton wrapper on top and seal the edges well, using more water if necessary. Set aside. Repeat the wonton-filling process until you are out of the filling or wontons. Preheat the panini press.

4. Place wontons on panini press and gently close the lid. Cook for 3–5 minutes or until wontons are crisp.

5. Remove from press and serve warm with a side of sour cream and Salsa (see Chapter 19 for recipe).

INGREDIENTS | **SERVES 2**

5–8 jalapeño peppers

10 wonton wrappers

½ cup grated Cheddar cheese

4 strips bacon, cooked and crumbled

Roasted Jalapeño Popper Wontons

Jalapeño poppers really aren't a portable food until you use your panini grill to press them inside of a wonton.

1. Preheat the panini press. Place the jalapeño peppers on panini press and close lid. Cook for 3–5 minutes. Remove from press and place on a cutting board. Scrape off any black char marks and cut into slices. Remove seeds and stems.

2. On a wonton wrapper, add a slice of jalapeño pepper, a pinch of Cheddar cheese, and some of the bacon. Make sure all the ingredients are small enough to fit inside the wonton. Wet the edges of the wonton wrapper with your finger or a basting brush. Lay another wonton wrapper on top and seal the edges well, using more water as necessary. Set aside. Repeat the wonton-filling process until you are out of the filling or wontons.

3. Place wontons on panini press and gently close the lid. Cook for 3–5 minutes or until wontons are crisp.

4. Remove from press and serve warm.

Sweet Potato Wontons

These delicious wontons are served with a brown butter sage sauce.

INGREDIENTS | SERVES 4

1 sweet potato
2 tablespoons butter, plus ¼ cup
½ cup Parmesan cheese
¼ teaspoon cinnamon
⅛ teaspoon nutmeg
20 wonton wrappers
1 tablespoon fresh sage
1 teaspoon lemon juice

1. Preheat the oven to 400°F. Bake the sweet potato for about 45 minutes. Remove from oven and set aside to cool. When it's cool enough, peel the skin off and discard.

2. In a bowl, add the sweet potato, 2 tablespoons butter, Parmesan cheese, cinnamon, and nutmeg and mix well. On a wonton wrapper, add a spoonful of the potato mixture and wet the edges with your finger or a basting brush. Lay another wonton wrapper on top and seal the edges well, using more water as necessary. Set aside. Repeat the wonton filling process until you are out of the filling or wontons. Preheat the panini press.

3. Place wontons on panini press and gently close the lid. Cook for 3–5 minutes or until wontons are crisp. Remove from press and set aside.

4. To make brown butter sage sauce, melt ¼ cup butter in a saucepan over medium heat and whisk while cooking until slightly brown (about 1 minute). Chop the fresh sage and add it to the butter with the lemon Juice. Mix well and pour over wontons.

20 wonton wrappers
1 cup Pesto Sauce (see Chapter 19)
1 tomato, chopped
¼ cup grated mozzarella cheese

Tomato Pesto Wontons

This recipe is an Italian-Asian recipe fusion, and it's wrapped in a bite-sized package.

1. On a wonton wrapper, add a spoonful of pesto, a piece of tomato, and pinch of shredded mozzarella cheese. Wet the edges with your finger or a basting brush and lay another wonton wrapper on top. Seal the edges well, using more water as necessary. Repeat wonton-filling process until you are out of the filling or wontons. Preheat the panini press.

2. Place wontons on panini press and gently close the lid.

3. Cook for 3–5 minutes or until wontons are crisp.

4. Remove from press and serve with a cup of tomato sauce for dipping.

Options

If you're in a rush and don't have time to fill wontons ingredient by ingredient, assembly line style, there is a quicker way to get it done. Put the pesto, the tomato, and the mozzarella cheese in a food processor and give it a quick chop—just enough to dice up the tomato and mix the ingredients. Now you can add a spoonful of the mixture onto the wontons, and you'll save some time.

INGREDIENTS | SERVES 4

2 tablespoons olive oil

2 tablespoons minced garlic

2 small zucchini, diced

1 onion, finely chopped

½ eggplant, diced

20 wonton wrappers

¼ cup goat cheese

Grilled Vegetable Wontons

*Crispy wontons go great with any grilled vegetables.
See what's in your fridge and try other vegetables too.
How about mushrooms, onions, and peppers?*

1. Pour the olive oil into a preheated frying pan and
   add the garlic, zucchini, onion, and eggplant. Cook
   for 4–6 minutes and remove from heat. Cool for
   about 5 minutes.

2. On a wonton wrapper, add a spoonful of the filling
   and a little goat cheese. Wet the edges with your
   finger or a basting brush and lay another wonton
   wrapper on top. Seal the edges well, using more
   water as necessary. Set aside. Repeat the wonton-
   filling process until you are out of the filling or
   wontons. Preheat the panini press.

3. Place wontons on panini press and gently close
   the lid. Cook for 3–5 minutes or until wontons are
   crisp.

4. Remove from press and serve warm.

CHAPTER 18

Beyond Sandwiches

1 pound medium shrimp, peeled and deveined

3 tablespoons olive oil

2 tablespoons minced garlic

1 tablespoon chili powder

1 teaspoon Worcestershire sauce

1 teaspoon lemon juice

Garlic Shrimp

This meal can be made in only a few minutes if you buy your shrimp peeled and deveined. Use any leftovers for a shrimp salad panini for lunch the next day.

1. In a bowl combine the shrimp, olive oil, garlic, chili powder, Worcestershire sauce, and lemon juice. Marinate for about 10 minutes. Preheat the panini press.

2. Pour contents of bowl on panini press.

3. Close lid and cook for 2–4 minutes. Remove from press and serve.

2 Vidalia onions

4 tablespoons olive oil

Salt and pepper, to taste

½ cup Steakhouse Dipping Sauce (see Chapter 19)

Grilled Onion Lollypops

You can't beat an onion on a stick.

1. Peel and slice each Vidalia onion about ½" thick. Jab a shish kebab skewer through each onion slice so that it looks like a lollypop.

2. Drizzle with olive oil and sprinkle with salt and pepper. Place on panini press, close lid, and cook for 3–5 minutes.

3. Remove from press and serve with Steakhouse Dipping Sauce.

1 pound medium shrimp, peeled and deveined

2 tablespoons lime juice

2 tablespoons rice vinegar

2 tablespoons Dijon mustard

2 tablespoons honey

2 cloves garlic

¼ teaspoon hot pepper flakes

¼ cup olive oil

Honey Shelf Life

Honey never goes bad. If honey solidifies, run the jar under some hot water and it'll be good as new.

Honey Lime Shrimp

The shrimp will actually start cooking in lime juice because of the citric acid. Don't let them marinate for more than 10 minutes.

1. In a bowl combine the shrimp, lime juice, rice vinegar, mustard, honey, garlic, hot pepper flakes, and olive oil. Marinate for about 10 minutes. Preheat the panini press.

2. Pour contents of bowl on panini press.

3. Close lid and cook for 2–4 minutes. Remove from press and serve.

1 pound boneless pork chops

1 red onion

1 red bell pepper

8 cherry tomatoes

8 crimini mushrooms

½ cup Pesto Sauce (see Chapter 19)

Pork Pesto Shish Kebabs

If making the Pesto Sauce specifically for this dish, add some water to the mix. The pork will absorb more of the flavor while it sits in the marinade this way.

1. Cut pork chops, red onion, red pepper into 1" cubes and place in a bowl along with the cherry tomatoes and crimini mushrooms. Add the Pesto Sauce and mix well. Marinate for about 1 hour in the refrigerator.

2. Preheat the panini press. Skewer the shish kebab pieces onto 6–8 skewers and place on panini press. Cook for 4–6 minutes with lid closed.

3. Remove from press and serve warm.

INGREDIENTS | SERVES 1

1 swordfish steak
1 celery rib
1 bell pepper
6 cherry tomatoes
2 tablespoons olive oil
½ cup Pesto Sauce (see Chapter 19)
Salt and pepper, to taste

Pesto Swordfish Kebabs

You could also use a tuna steak or halibut for this recipe. Any meaty whitefish will taste just as good.

1. Cut swordfish, celery, and bell pepper into 1" cubes and place in a bowl along with the cherry tomatoes. Add the remaining ingredients and mix well. Preheat the panini press.

2. Skewer the shish kebab pieces onto 2 skewers and place on panini press. Cook for 4–6 minutes with lid closed.

3. Remove from press and serve warm.

Soak Your Skewers

In order to avoid charring, soak wooden skewers in water for about an hour before you use them. Metal skewers are a great investment if you plan on making shish kebabs regularly.

INGREDIENTS | SERVES 2

1 Cornish game hen
1 tablespoon chili powder
1 teaspoon thyme
1 tablespoon onion powder
1 tablespoon garlic powder
1 teaspoon white pepper
1 teaspoon salt

Butterflied Cornish Game Hen

Your panini press can be used to make all sorts of interesting meals. You don't have to eat sandwiches every day!

1. Using a pair of kitchen scissors, cut the spine out of a Cornish game hen by cutting about ½" to the right of the spine and then ½" to the left of the spine. Remove spine and open up the hen so that it lays flat. Tuck wings behind the body so that the entire hen is flat.

2. In a bowl combine remaining ingredients and stir to mix. Rub entire hen with spices. Really massage the rub into the bird. Preheat the panini press.

3. Place hen on panini press and make sure it's laying flat. Close the lid and cook for 15 minutes.

4. Remove from press and serve warm.

Cilantro Lime Kebabs

INGREDIENTS | SERVES 1

1 chicken breast
1 red onion
1 red bell pepper
8 cherry tomatoes
¼ cup lime juice
2 tablespoons minced garlic
1 tablespoon cilantro
2 tablespoons olive oil
Salt and pepper, to taste

Cilantro and lime make for a tangy marinade with a Tex-Mex flair. This recipe is basically chicken fajitas on a stick.

1. Cut chicken breast, red onion, and bell pepper into 1" cubes and place in a bowl along with the cherry tomatoes. Add lime juice, garlic, cilantro, olive oil, salt, and pepper and mix well. Marinate for about 1 hour in the refrigerator.

2. Preheat the panini press. Skewer the shish kebab pieces onto 2 or 3 skewers and place on panini press. Cook for 4–6 minutes with lid closed.

3. Remove from press and serve warm.

Barbecue Chicken Shish Kebabs

INGREDIENTS | SERVES 2

2 boneless chicken cutlets
1 red onion
1 red bell pepper
8 cherry tomatoes
8 crimini mushrooms
½ cup barbecue sauce
Salt and pepper, to taste

Cutting all the pieces the same size helps everything cook evenly.

1. Cut chicken breast, red onion, and bell pepper into 1" cubes and place in a bowl along with the cherry tomatoes and crimini mushrooms. Add barbecue sauce, salt, and pepper and mix well. Marinate for about 1 hour in the refrigerator.

2. Preheat the panini press. Skewer the shish kebab pieces onto 4–6 skewers and place on panini press. Cook for 4–6 minutes with lid closed.

3. Remove from press and serve warm.

Garlic Pork Shish Kebabs

INGREDIENTS | SERVES 2

1 pound boneless pork chops

1 red onion

1 orange bell pepper

8 cherry tomatoes

8 crimini mushrooms

3 tablespoons olive oil

2 tablespoons minced garlic

Salt and pepper, to taste

Pork cutlets can be used instead of boneless pork chops, but they usually aren't as thick. Pork chops are much easier to cut into cubes.

1. Cut pork chops, red onion, and bell pepper into 1" cubes and place in a bowl along with the cherry tomatoes and crimini mushrooms. Add olive oil, garlic, salt, and pepper and mix well. Marinate for about 1 hour in the refrigerator.

2. Preheat the panini press. Skewer the shish kebab pieces onto 4–6 skewers and place on panini press. Cook for 4–6 minutes with lid closed.

3. Remove from press and serve warm.

Teriyaki Shish Kebabs

INGREDIENTS | SERVES 2

2 boneless chicken cutlets

1 red onion

1 red bell pepper

8 zucchini wedges

12–15 pineapple chunks

8 crimini mushrooms

½ cup teriyaki sauce

Fresh pineapple almost tastes like a different fruit when compared to those rings you get out of a can.

1. Cut chicken, red onion, bell pepper, zucchini, and pineapple into 1" cubes and place in a bowl along with the crimini mushrooms. Add the teriyaki sauce and mix well. Marinate for about 1 hour in the refrigerator.

2. Preheat the panini press. Skewer the shish kebab pieces onto 4–6 skewers and place on panini press. Cook for 4–6 minutes with lid closed.

3. Remove from press and serve warm.

Orange Ginger Beef Shish Kebabs

INGREDIENTS | SERVES 2

1 pound flank steak
1 onion
1 red bell pepper
8 broccoli stalks
8 crimini mushrooms
2 tablespoons soy sauce
¼ cup orange juice
1 tablespoon peanut oil
1 teaspoon minced ginger
1 tablespoon rice wine

These kebabs are a great addition to any barbecue. It doesn't always have to be about hamburgers and hot dogs.

1. Cut flank steak, onion, red pepper, and broccoli into 1" cubes and place in a bowl along with the crimini mushrooms. Add soy sauce, orange juice, peanut oil, ginger, and rice wine and mix well. Marinate for about 1 hour in the refrigerator.

2. Preheat the panini press. Skewer the shish kebab pieces onto 6–8 skewers and place on panini press. Cook for 4–6 minutes with lid closed.

3. Remove from press and serve warm.

Flank Worcestershire Shish Kebabs

INGREDIENTS | SERVES 2

1 pound flank steak
1 red onion
1 red bell pepper
8 zucchini wedges
8 crimini mushrooms
½ cup soy sauce
2 tablespoons Worcestershire sauce
⅓ cup canola oil

You can add any vegetable that grills well to your shish kebabs. Get creative and experiment with whatever you have on hand.

1. Cut flank steak, red onion, bell pepper, and zucchini into 1" cubes and place in a bowl along with the crimini mushrooms. Add the soy sauce, Worcestershire sauce, and canola oil and mix well. Marinate for about 1 hour in the refrigerator.

2. Preheat the panini press. Skewer the shish kebab pieces onto 6–8 skewers and place on panini press. Cook for 4–6 minutes with lid closed.

3. Remove from press and serve warm.

Honey Lime Shish Kebabs

Fresh limes really make a big difference in the flavor of these kebabs. If limes are out of season, then feel free to use bottled lime juice.

INGREDIENTS | SERVES 2

2 boneless chicken cutlets

1 red onion

1 red bell pepper

8 cherry tomatoes

8 crimini mushrooms

¼ cup olive oil

2 tablespoons lime juice

2 tablespoons rice wine vinegar

2 tablespoons Dijon mustard

2 tablespoons honey

2 tablespoons minced garlic

¼ teaspoon hot pepper flakes

1. Cut chicken, red onion, and bell pepper into 1" cubes and place in a bowl along with the cherry tomatoes and crimini mushrooms. Add olive oil, lime juice, rice wine vinegar, Dijon mustard, honey, garlic, and hot pepper flakes and mix well. Marinate for about 1 hour in the refrigerator.

2. Preheat the panini press. Skewer the shish kebab pieces onto 4–6 skewers and place on panini press. Cook for 4–6 minutes with lid closed.

3. Remove from press and serve warm.

Lemon Garlic Shish Kebabs

Be sure to wash and pat dry all the ingredients with a paper towel before adding them to the marinade.

INGREDIENTS | SERVES 2

2 boneless chicken cutlets

1 red onion

1 red bell pepper

8 zucchini wedges

8 white mushrooms

¼ cup canola oil

¼ cup lemon juice

3 tablespoons minced garlic

½ teaspoon black pepper

1 teaspoon tarragon

1. Cut chicken, red onion, bell pepper, and zucchini into 1" pieces and place in a bowl along with the mushrooms. Add the canola oil, lemon juice, garlic, black pepper, and tarragon and mix well. Marinate for about 1 hour in the refrigerator.

2. Preheat the panini press. Skewer the shish kebab pieces onto 6–8 skewers and place on panini press. Cook for 4–6 minutes with lid closed.

3. Remove from press and serve warm.

½ cup canola oil
4 cloves garlic
½ cup lemon juice
½ cup tahini
3 tablespoons water
1 teaspoon salt
·1 pound London broil steak
1 red onion
1 red bell pepper
8 zucchini wedges
8 crimini mushrooms

Shish Kebabs with Tahini Marinade

The thickness of London broil makes it perfectly suited for the cube shapes of shish kebab.

1. In a food processor combine canola oil, garlic, lemon juice, tahini, water, and salt and mix until well blended.

2. Cut London broil, red onion, bell pepper, and zucchini into 1" cubes and place in a bowl along with the crimini mushrooms. Add the tahini mixture and mix well. Marinate for about 1 hour in the refrigerator.

3. Preheat the panini press. Skewer the shish kebab pieces onto 6–8 skewers and place on panini press. Cook for 4–6 minutes with lid closed.

4. Remove from press and serve warm.

¼ cup whiskey

¼ cup soy sauce

¼ cup honey Dijon mustard

¼ cup brown sugar

2 tablespoons lime juice

¼ cup sesame oil

3 tablespoons minced garlic

1 teaspoon pepper

1 pound flank steak

1 red onion

1 red bell pepper

8 zucchini wedges

1 corn on the cob

8 crimini mushrooms

Whiskey Shish Kebabs

An old sock would probably taste good with this whiskey and soy marinade. But you should probably stick to steak and vegetables.

1. In a bowl combine whiskey, soy sauce, mustard, brown sugar, lime juice, sesame oil, garlic, and pepper and mix until well blended.

2. Cut flank steak, red onion, bell pepper, zucchini, and corn on the cob into 1" pieces and place in a bowl along with the crimini mushrooms. Add the whiskey-soy marinade and mix well. Marinate for about 1 hour in the refrigerator.

3. Preheat the panini press. Skewer the shish kebab pieces onto 6–8 skewers and place on panini press. Cook for 4–6 minutes with lid closed.

4. Remove from press and serve warm.

1 pound boneless pork chops
1 red onion
1 red bell pepper
8 zucchini wedges
8 white mushrooms
¼ cup olive oil
¼ cup balsamic vinegar
2 tablespoons brown sugar
¼ cup minced onions
Salt and pepper, to taste

Shish Kebabs with Balsamic Marinade

Kebabs make great party food because you can prepare them in advance. When the guests arrive, all you have to do is fire up the panini press.

1. Cut pork chop, red onion, bell pepper, and zucchini into 1" pieces and place in a bowl along with the mushrooms. Add the olive oil, balsamic vinegar, brown sugar, minced onions, salt, and pepper and mix well. Marinate for about 1 hour in the refrigerator.

2. Preheat the panini press. Skewer the shish kebab pieces onto 6–8 skewers and place on panini press. Cook for 4–6 minutes with lid closed.

3. Remove from press and serve warm.

2 boneless chicken cutlets

1 red onion

1 red bell pepper

8 zucchini wedges

8 white mushrooms

¼ cup olive oil

¼ cup lemon juice

1 tablespoon oregano

1 teaspoon rosemary

Salt and pepper, to taste

Rosemary Shish Kebabs

Fresh rosemary is much more flavorful than dried rosemary from your spice rack. If you have space in your vegetable garden, rosemary would make a nice addition.

1. Cut chicken, red onion, bell pepper, and zucchini into 1" pieces and place in a bowl along with the mushrooms. Add the olive oil, lemon juice, oregano, rosemary, salt, and pepper and mix well. Marinate for about 1 hour in the refrigerator.

2. Preheat the panini press. Skewer the shish kebab pieces onto 4–6 skewers and place on panini press. Cook for 4–6 minutes with lid closed.

3. Remove from press and serve warm.

Garlic Sticks

If you can find a pizzeria that sells pizza dough, then you'll be all set. It's just flour and water, but there's magic in there.

INGREDIENTS | SERVES 2

1 8-ounce pizza dough
3 tablespoons butter
3 tablespoons minced garlic

Variations
Add a little Parmesan cheese to the garlic butter before spreading it on the dough.

1. Preheat the panini press. Knead the pizza dough and roll into long thin strips.

2. Melt the butter in the microwave for about 30 seconds and add the garlic. Using a basting brush, coat the dough strips with the garlic butter. Place on panini press, close lid, and cook for 3–5 minutes.

3. Remove from panini press and serve warm with a side of tomato sauce for dunking.

Grilled Asparagus with Garlic

Asparagus is a nutritionally dense green vegetable and an excellent source of folic acid.

INGREDIENTS | SERVES 2

10–20 asparagus stalks
3 tablespoons olive oil
1 tablespoon minced garlic

Asparagus
Asparagus stalks can sometimes taste a little woody. If you take a vegetable peeler and scrape off a little bit before cooking, they will taste almost as tender as the flower side.

1. Preheat the panini press. Place asparagus stalks on panini press and drizzle with olive oil. Add the garlic on top and close the lid.

2. Cook for 3–5 minutes and remove from press.

3. Serve warm.

2 small zucchini

1 peeled potato

1 onion, chopped

4 cloves garlic, minced

¼ cup Parmesan cheese

2 eggs

Salt and pepper, to taste

Zucchini Potato Pancakes

Zucchini and potato pancakes come out nice and crispy when you cook them in a panini press. Just mind the ridges.

1. Using the shredding disc on your food processor, chop up the zucchini and the potato. Empty the food processor into a towel and squeeze out all the extra liquid over the sink.

2. Preheat the panini press. Place the onion and garlic in a mixing bowl. Add the Parmesan cheese, eggs, and salt and pepper to taste. Mix well and make sure eggs are beaten. Add the zucchini and potatoes and stir until evenly coated. Form into hamburger-sized patties and place on panini press.

3. Close lid and cook for 4–6 minutes. Remove from press and serve with a dollop of sour cream.

Potato Chip Chicken Kebabs

If you like the taste of potato chips, you'll love this recipe. The potato chips are the breading for the chicken strips on this panini.

1. Preheat the panini press. Crack the egg in a bowl and beat it. Place the crushed potato chips in another bowl. Cut chicken cutlets into strips and skewer with shish kebab sticks. Dip chicken into egg and then into potato chip crumbs to bread them.

2. Place the breaded chicken strips on panini press, close lid, and cook for 3–5 minutes.

3. Remove from press and serve warm with a small bowl of honey mustard for dipping.

Variations

Although this is a kebab recipe, you can enjoy potato chip chicken in a panini sandwich too. Prepare the chicken the same way, except skip the shish kebab skewers and put the chicken between two slices of bread with some honey mustard.

10–20 asparagus stalks
3 tablespoons olive oil
Juice of 1 lemon

Lemon Grilled Asparagus

You can also let the asparagus marinate in a container with the olive oil and lemon juice before grilling them on the panini press.

1. Preheat the panini press. Place asparagus stalks on panini press and drizzle with olive oil. Squeeze the lemon juice on top and close the lid.

2. Cook for 3–5 minutes and remove from press.

3. Serve warm.

Asparagus

The name "asparagus" is derived from a Greek word meaning "sprout." This makes sense because the asparagus that you buy at the supermarket also started out as a sprout. If it wasn't picked, it would have grown into a large fern-like bush.

CHAPTER 19

Sauces, Condiments, and Spreads for Panini

⅓ cup pine nuts

2–3 cups basil leaves

⅔ cup extra-virgin olive oil

2–3 cloves garlic

⅓ cup Parmesan cheese

Salt and pepper, to taste

Pesto Sauce

Pesto is a popular sauce made from basil leaves, garlic, and pine nuts. It can also be used as a condiment on panini sandwiches.

1. In a food processor, chop up pine nuts and set aside.

2. Add basil leaves and olive oil to food processor and use the pulse setting until all the leaves are chopped.

3. Add garlic, pine nuts, and Parmesan cheese and continue processing until smooth.

4. Add salt and pepper and mix well.

5. Remove from food processor and store in refrigerator for up to a week.

Pesto Variations

Roasted pumpkin seeds can be used as a substitute for the pine nuts. Also, try replacing the basil with either spinach or arugula.

⅓ cup pine nuts

2 cups pitted green or Kalamata olives

⅔ cup extra-virgin olive oil

2–3 cloves garlic

Salt and pepper, to taste

Olive Pesto

Olive pesto is normally used in appetizers like bruschetta, as a pizza topping, or even as a ravioli filling. But add it to a dull panini sandwich and you'll be looking for seconds.

1. In a food processor, chop up pine nuts and set aside.

2. Add olives and olive oil to food processor and use the pulse setting until everything is chopped.

3. Add garlic and pine nuts and continue processing until smooth.

4. Add salt and pepper and mix well.

5. Remove from food processor and store in refrigerator for up to a week.

INGREDIENTS | SERVES 2

1 bulb garlic
2 tablespoons olive oil

Roasted Garlic

Roasting garlic takes away the strong, bitter taste of raw garlic and gives it a milder, nutty flavor.

1. Preheat oven to 400°F.

2. Peel away the papery outer layers of garlic skin, but do not expose cloves. Cut about ¼" off of the top of cloves so that you can see individual cloves of garlic. Drizzle with olive oil and wrap in aluminum foil. Make sure that the garlic bulb stays upright inside the foil.

3. Move to oven and bake for about 40 minutes or until cloves are soft. Let garlic cool until it can be handled but has not gotten cold.

4. Separate each clove from the bulb and squeeze the roasted garlic out with your fingers.

5. Store in refrigerator for up to a week.

Roasted Garlic Panini

Italian bread and roasted garlic don't need any other ingredients to be enjoyed in a panini. Just put the garlic between two slices of bread and place it on a preheated panini press for a few minutes. No amount of brushing your teeth will get rid of the garlic breath—but it's worth it.

Garlic Mayonnaise

INGREDIENTS | SERVES 4

3–4 cloves Roasted Garlic (see recipe in this chapter)
1 cup mayonnaise

Garlic Mayonnaise is very simple to make, and yet it adds great flavor to panini sandwiches. It's definitely much better than adding garlic and mayonnaise separately.

1. In a food processor, combine roasted garlic and mayonnaise.

2. Mix for about 1 minute or until well blended.

3. Remove from food processor and store in refrigerator for up to a week.

Horseradish Mayonnaise

INGREDIENTS | SERVES 4

½ cup mayonnaise
1 tablespoon horseradish
1 teaspoon lemon juice
Pinch black pepper

Save this recipe for when you make a roast beef. The paninis will be fantastic.

1. In a food processor, blend all ingredients until smooth.

2. Store in the refrigerator for up to a week.

INGREDIENTS | SERVES 1

1 bell pepper

Roasted Peppers

Roasting peppers is a time-consuming task, but it's worth the effort. Whether you're using bell peppers, poblano peppers, or even chili peppers, they'll taste a lot better when they've been roasted.

1. Preheat the panini press. Place pepper on panini press and leave open.

2. Grill until pepper turns black, then rotate pepper a quarter turn and repeat until entire pepper is blackened.

3. Place roasted pepper in a paper bag and fold closed. Wait 15–20 minutes, then place pepper on a cutting board.

4. Scrape off the blackened skin and discard. Cut into slices and discard the seed pod.

5. Store in refrigerator for up to a week.

Poblano Chili Sauce

INGREDIENTS | SERVES 4

1 white onion
2 cups roasted poblano peppers
1–3 garlic cloves
2 tablespoons oregano
2 tablespoons honey
Salt and pepper, to taste

This chili sauce is a lot of work, but it's worth the trouble. Make a double batch and freeze the rest for next time.

1. In a food processor, add onion and chop.

2. Add roasted poblano peppers, garlic, and oregano and continue chopping.

3. Add honey, salt, and pepper.

4. Chop until well blended.

5. Store in refrigerator for up to a week.

Hummus

INGREDIENTS | SERVES 4

1 can chickpeas (garbanzo beans), drained
3 teaspoons lemon juice
1½ tablespoons tahini
2 garlic cloves
½ teaspoon salt
⅛ cup olive oil

Hummus is a popular Middle Eastern dip that's made with chickpeas. It also goes great on panini sandwiches.

1. Combine all ingredients in a food processor and blend until smooth.

2. Store in refrigerator for up to a week.

What Is Tahini?

Tahini is a ground sesame seed paste that's similar to peanut butter. It's usually found in the refrigerated section of your supermarket near the hummus. You may also find it in dehydrated form at health food stores or premium markets.

Olive Tapenade

INGREDIENTS | SERVES 4

2 cups pitted Kalamata olives
1 tablespoon capers
1 teaspoon lemon juice
1 tablespoon olive oil
½ teaspoon anchovy paste

Tapenade is a very popular spread in Mediterranean homes. It's made from olives and it's very easy to make.

1. Combine all ingredients in a food processor and pulse a few times. Ingredients should look they have been given a rough chop.

2. Store in refrigerator for up to a week.

Salsa

INGREDIENTS | SERVES 6

3 chopped tomatoes
½ cup chopped onion
1 jalapeño pepper
2 cloves garlic
1 lime
2 tablespoons cilantro
Salt and pepper, to taste

It's more convenient to use store-bought salsa, but once you taste this homemade version, you may never buy another jar again. Salsa is normally used for dipping chips, but you can also dip a panini into salsa. It can also be used as a condiment.

1. Combine all ingredients in a food processor and give them a rough chop.

2. Store in refrigerator for up to a week.

Guacamole

INGREDIENTS | SERVES 1

4 avocados, peeled, pitted, and roughly chopped
2 tablespoons lime juice
½ teaspoon salt
½ onion
½ cup diced tomatoes
2 cloves garlic

This dip is not only delicious, but it's also fun to say out loud while you're making it. Guacamole!

1. Combine all ingredients in a food processor and blend until smooth.

2. Store in refrigerator for up to a week.

Chipotle Mayonnaise

INGREDIENTS | SERVES 1

1 cup mayonnaise
2 tablespoons chipotle chilies in adobo sauce
1 teaspoon cilantro
1 teaspoon lime juice
Salt and pepper, to taste

This mayonnaise will make anything that you put it on taste like it came from south of the border.

1. Combine all ingredients in a food processor and blend until smooth.

2. Store in refrigerator for up to a week.

Where to Find Chipotles

You should be able to find chipotles in adobo sauce at most premium supermarkets or ethnic grocery stores. The Goya brand is very popular and will be most widely available.

Hummus with Pine Nuts

INGREDIENTS | SERVES 1

3 cloves garlic

1 can chickpeas, drained

½ cup tahini

⅛ cup lemon juice

¼ cup water

⅛ cup olive oil

Salt, to taste

¼ cup pine nuts

There are so many varieties of hummus that you'll never grow tired of it.

1. Combine all ingredients in a food processor and blend until smooth.

2. Store in refrigerator for up to a week.

Roasted Red Pepper Hummus

INGREDIENTS | SERVES 4

1 can chickpeas or garbanzo beans, drained

3 teaspoons lemon juice

1½ tablespoons tahini

2 garlic cloves

½ teaspoon salt

⅛ cup olive oil

¼ cup roasted red peppers

Roasted red peppers not only make this hummus taste great, but they also give it an attractive pink color.

1. Combine all ingredients in a food processor and blend until smooth.

2. Store in refrigerator for up to a week.

Roasted Corn Salsa

INGREDIENTS | SERVES 6

½ cup corn kernels
1 tablespoon olive oil
3 chopped tomatoes
½ cup chopped onion
1 jalapeño pepper
2 cloves garlic
Juice of 1 lime
2 tablespoons cilantro
Salt and pepper, to taste
¼ cup canned black beans, drained

Once you taste this, you may not want to save this salsa for a panini.

1. Preheat the panini press. Pour the corn on panini press and drizzle with olive oil. Close lid and cook for 2–4 minutes. Remove from press and set aside.

2. Combine all ingredients in a food processor and give them a rough chop.

3. Store in refrigerator for up to a week.

Variations
Try substituting poblano peppers for the jalapeños for a more smoky flavor.

Spinach Pesto

INGREDIENTS | SERVES 6

2 cups spinach
1 cup basil leaves
⅔ cup extra-virgin olive oil
2–3 cloves garlic
⅓ cup pine nuts
⅓ cup Parmesan cheese
Salt and pepper, to taste

Pesto can be made with many different ingredients, including spinach.

1. Combine all ingredients in a food processor and blend until smooth.

2. Store in refrigerator for up to a week.

Black Bean Pesto

This pesto is perfect for a Mexican panini.

1. Combine all ingredients in a food processor except the black beans and give them a rough chop.

2. Add the black beans to the chopped ingredients in a bowl and mix with a wooden spoon.

3. Store in refrigerator for up to a week.

Baba Ganoush

Give your panini a Middle Eastern flair by adding some baba ganoush.

1. Preheat the panini press. Brush eggplant with olive oil, place on panini press, close lid, and cook for 3–5 minutes. Remove eggplant from press and set aside.

2. Combine all ingredients in a food processor and give them a rough chop.

3. Store in refrigerator for up to a week.

Satay Sauce

INGREDIENTS | SERVES 6

10 ounces coconut milk
½ cup crunchy peanut butter
¼ cup finely chopped onion
1 tablespoon soy sauce
2 teaspoons brown sugar
½ teaspoon red pepper flakes

Here's a quick and easy satay sauce that goes great with chicken.

1. Combine all ingredients in a saucepan over medium heat.

2. Bring to a boil while stirring.

3. Serve warm.

Creole Mayonnaise

INGREDIENTS | SERVES 6

½ white onion
1 cup mayonnaise
2 tablespoons lemon juice
1 teaspoon hot sauce
1 teaspoon Cajun seasoning
1 teaspoon black pepper

You can't make a po' boy sandwich without Creole Mayonnaise. Try it with any panini that you want to jazz up.

1. In a food processor, chop the onion. Then add the rest of the ingredients and chop again until smooth.

2. Remove from food processor and store in fridge for up to a week.

Cajun Seasoning

Cajun seasoning is usually a mixture of salt and a variety of bold spices. Each brand contains a blend of spices that are a bit different but most contain garlic, onion, pepper, cayenne pepper, and chili powder.

Cilantro Lime Mayonnaise

INGREDIENTS | SERVES 1

1 cup mayonnaise
1 cup fresh cilantro
3 tablespoons lime juice
2 cloves garlic
1 teaspoon Dijon mustard
Dash of hot sauce

You can give any panini some Tex-Mex flair by adding some Cilantro Lime Mayonnaise.

1. Place all ingredients in a food processor and mix until well blended.

2. Store for up to a week in the refrigerator.

Steakhouse Dipping Sauce

INGREDIENTS | SERVES 1

½ cup mayonnaise
2 teaspoons ketchup
1 teaspoon horseradish
¼ teaspoon paprika
½ teaspoon garlic powder
¼ teaspoon oregano
Salt and pepper, to taste

This dipping sauce is perfect for grilled onions or onion rings, but it's also really good on panini sandwiches.

1. Place all ingredients in a food processor and mix until well blended.

2. Store for up to a week in the refrigerator.

APPENDIX A

Glossary

ANCHOVIES: Small silver fish, usually packed in brine, that are popular in Mediterranean cuisine.

ARUGULA: A peppery salad green, popular in Italian cuisine. Also know as rocket, roquette, rugula, and rucola.

BALSAMIC VINEGAR: A rich and slightly sweet vinegar that is popular in Italian cuisine.

BROCCOLI RAAB: A bitter green that is botanically related to turnips. Also known as cime di rapa and rappi.

CAJUN SEASONING: Usually composed of salt, cayenne pepper, garlic, onion powder, black pepper, chili powder, thyme, and basil.

CHUTNEY: A cooked condiment made of fruits or vegetables that are cooked in vinegar with sugar and spices. Popular in Indian cuisine.

CRIMINI MUSHROOMS: Small brown Italian mushrooms. Crimini are baby portobellos, sometimes sold as baby bellas.

DIJON MUSTARD: A strong mustard that originated in the Dijon region of France.

FETA CHEESE: A white cheese with small holes. Popular in Greek cuisine.

FONTINA CHEESE: A soft cheese with an earthy taste; made from cow's milk.

GORGONZOLA CHEESE: A veined Italian blue cheese.

KALAMATA OLIVES: Olives from Kalamata region of Greece. Also known as Greek olives.

LUMP CRABMEAT: Crabmeat that has been extracted from the crab's shell.

MASCARPONE CHEESE: A creamy cheese made from crème fraîche.

MONTEREY JACK CHEESE: A semihard cheese made from cow's milk. Popular in Mexican cuisine.

MOZZARELLA CHEESE: Semisoft white cheese made from the milk of the domestic water buffalo or from cow's milk.

PANCETTA: Seasoned salt-cured pork belly. Similar to bacon.

NUTELLA: A popular brand of chocolate hazelnut spread that has been around since the 1940s.

PARMESAN CHEESE: Slightly bitter Italian hard cheese made from cow's milk.

PESTO: An Italian sauce that's usually made with basil, garlic, olive oil, and pine nuts, but there are many variations.

PORTOBELLO MUSHROOMS: Large brown Italian mushrooms.

PROSCIUTTO: A dry-cured ham usually made from a pig or wild boar's hind leg or thigh.

ROQUEFORT CHEESE: A white pungent cheese with veins of green that is made from sheep's milk.

ROMAINE LETTUCE: A popular variety of salad green that is very crisp and tender.

SARDINES: Small oily fish that are cooked and packed in cans of oil or water.

SHISH KEBAB: Cubes of marinated meat and vegetables that are skewered before cooking.

SKEWER: A metal or wood stick that is used to hold shish kebab ingredients together.

TAPENADE: A spread made of finely chopped olives, capers, anchovies, and olive oil. Usually served with bread or crackers.

WATERCRESS LETTUCE: A peppery salad green.

WORCESTERSHIRE SAUCE: A vinegar-based sauce that's used to flavor meats and cocktails.

Additional Resources

Bread Recipes

All Recipes
This site is a great place to start if you want to bake your own bread.
http://allrecipes.com//Recipes/bread

Bread Recipe
Another great bread recipe site. Be sure to try their muffins too.
http://bread-recipe.com

Cooking Bread
A small collection of fantastic bread recipes.
www.cookingbread.com

The Knead for Bread
This blog is loaded with recipes and mouth-watering photos.
www.thekneadforbread.com

Martha Stewart
Martha Stewart can do it all.
www.marthastewart.com/bread

Panini Press Manufacturers

Breville
You may already know that Breville makes juicers, toasters, and espresso makers, but they also make panini presses.
www.brevilleusa.com

Calphalon
They make nonstick pots and also nonstick panini presses.
www.calphalon.com

Cuisinart
Cuisinart is a trusted name when it comes to home appliances.
www.cuisinart.com

DeLonghi
DeLonghi makes gorgeous retro-styled panini presses.
www.shopdelonghi.com

George Foreman
Besides the George Foreman Fat Reducing Lean Mean Grilling Machine, the big man also makes a nice panini press.
www.georgeforemancooking.com

Hamilton Beach
Hamilton Beach sells over 35 million kitchen appliances each year.
www.hamiltonbeach.com

Krups
You've tried their coffee makers, now try their panini makers.
www.krupsusa.com

Sensio
Sensio's products offer a premium kitchen experience.
www.sensioinc.com

Villaware
Villaware appliances are well-made.
www.villaware.com

West Bend
West Bend has been around since 1911.
www.westbend.com

Ingredients

Nutella
The delicious hazelnut spread that's great for dessert panini.
www.nutellausa.com

Omaha Steaks
Omaha Steaks has a wide selection of gourmet meats and seafoods.
www.omahasteaks.com

Panera Bread
If you have a Panera Bread in your area, you'll enjoy their fresh-baked bread.
www.panerabread.com

Standard U.S./Metric Measurement Conversions

VOLUME CONVERSIONS

U.S. Volume Measure	Metric Equivalent
⅛ teaspoon	0.5 milliliters
¼ teaspoon	1 milliliters
½ teaspoon	2 milliliters
1 teaspoon	5 milliliters
½ tablespoon	7 milliliters
1 tablespoon (3 teaspoons)	15 milliliters
2 tablespoons (1 fluid ounce)	30 milliliters
¼ cup (4 tablespoons)	60 milliliters
⅓ cup	90 milliliters
½ cup (4 fluid ounces)	125 milliliters
⅔ cup	160 milliliters
¾ cup (6 fluid ounces)	180 milliliters
1 cup (16 tablespoons)	250 milliliters
1 pint (2 cups)	500 milliliters
1 quart (4 cups)	1 liter (about)

WEIGHT CONVERSIONS

U.S. Weight Measure	Metric Equivalent
½ ounce	15 grams
1 ounce	30 grams
2 ounces	60 grams
3 ounces	85 grams
¼ pound (4 ounces)	115 grams
½ pound (8 ounces)	225 grams
¾ pound (12 ounces)	340 grams
1 pound (16 ounces)	454 grams

OVEN TEMPERATURE CONVERSIONS

Degrees Fahrenheit	Degrees Celsius
200 degrees F	95 degrees C
250 degrees F	120 degrees C
275 degrees F	135 degrees C
300 degrees F	150 degrees C
325 degrees F	160 degrees C
350 degrees F	180 degrees C
375 degrees F	190 degrees C
400 degrees F	205 degrees C
425 degrees F	220 degrees C
450 degrees F	230 degrees C

BAKING PAN SIZES

American	Metric
8 x 1½ inch round baking pan	20 x 4 cm cake tin
9 x 1½ inch round baking pan	23 x 3.5 cm cake tin
11 x 7 x 1½ inch baking pan	28 x 18 x 4 cm baking tin
13 x 9 x 2 inch baking pan	30 x 20 x 5 cm baking tin
2 quart rectangular baking dish	30 x 20 x 3 cm baking tin
15 x 10 x 2 inch baking pan	30 x 25 x 2 cm baking tin (Swiss roll tin)
9 inch pie plate	22 x 4 or 23 x 4 cm pie plate
7 or 8 inch springform pan	18 or 20 cm springform or loose bottom cake tin
9 x 5 x 3 inch loaf pan	23 x 13 x 7 cm or 2 lb narrow loaf or pate tin
1½ quart casserole	1.5 litre casserole
2 quart casserole	2 litre casserole

Index

Note: Page numbers in **bold** indicate recipe category lists.

We Have
EVERYTHING®
on Anything!

The Everything® list spans a wide range of subjects, with more than 500 titles covering 25 different categories:

Business	History	Reference
Careers	Home Improvement	Religion
Children's Storybooks	Everything Kids	Self-Help
Computers	Languages	Sports & Fitness
Cooking	Music	Travel
Crafts and Hobbies	New Age	Wedding
Education/Schools	Parenting	Writing
Games and Puzzles	Personal Finance	
Health	Pets	